Dr. Charles Mutua Mulli

MY JOURNEY OF FAITH

*An Encounter with Christ
and How He Used Me to
Spread His Love to the Poor*

In 2003 I, a stranger to Mr. Mulli, sent him a letter offering to transport three of his children across Canada on the back of a modified tandem bike, creating awareness and raising funds for MCF. Three weeks later he replied, "After discussion with my wife, Esther, my biological family, and seeking God's will through prayer, I believe this to be the beginning of a lifetime partnership." We were amazed at the faith required to trust a complete stranger with his kids.

As you read *My Journey of Faith* you, too, will be amazed by his example of unwavering faith in God, inspired to trust God more in your own journey and motivated to put your faith into action.

Arvid Loewen
founder of GrandpasCan,
director with MCF Canada

❀ ❀ ❀

I highly recommend the amazing story of this man and wife of compassion and action. The wealthy, successful Mully family abandoned their earthly riches and social prestige so they could transform despair into radiant hope for the desperate broken street kids of Kenya. Though insane by earthly standards, they were totally sane by God's standards and very wise investors. Their riches now are not in money or land but in thousands of transformed lives in Kenya and beyond. The future, though not yet written, may be even greater than the past. I am highly honoured to be counted among their friend for many years.

Rev. Jack Hawkins
Minister at Large with OM Canada

❀ ❀ ❀

Dr. Charles Mulli's 25th anniversary account, *My Journey of Faith*, is a remarkable testimony to God's power and God's grace in every situation. The unspeakable things Charles Mulli saw and endured were overcome when he accepted Christ and gave his life to God. Charles Mulli's heart for the children who walk the streets and endure hunger, exploitation and fear, just like he did as a young boy, changed the heart of Africa and beyond. Dr. Mulli's complete surrender to God and His will allowed Dr. Mulli to be blessed beyond his expectations. There were miracles, one after another, solely because Dr. Mulli believed that anything was possible through Christ. This book is a testimony to us all. It is a walk of faith all of us as Christians benefit from reading. *My Journey of Faith* brings Dr. Mulli's journey of faith alive and real to all of us. His story leaves us with inspiration to carry on in tough times because God is real and He is always with us.

Joy Smith, B.Ed., M.Ed.
founder and president of The Joy Smith Foundation

Many people dream of doing something that matters, of making a difference in the world, of impacting lives. The incredible truth about Charles' life is that he *is* actually doing something that matters; he *is* making a real difference in this world and he is impacting lives in a most profound way. And how beautiful that Mully Children's Family all began with a simply act of human kindness and an awareness of those who were suffering in Charles' community. *My Journey of Faith* is a very *human* story. It is a story of suffering and triumph, of compassion and celebration, of self-sacrifice and trust in God.

Marina Hofman Willard, Ph.D.
Palm Beach Atlantic University

My wife, Erna, and I visited the Mully orphanage several years ago. We were moved by the love and care for the homeless children of Africa. For us, this book completes the story of why the orphanage exists. Charles Mulli, the founder, tells it with candour and honesty. We read of his call from God to leave his successful business career to rescue children from abject poverty and abuse. The lasting transformation of thousands of children leaves a legacy that glorifies God.

Herb and Erna Buller
Buller Foundation

My Journey Of Faith gives us a personal insight into the challenges Charles Mulli has overcome in his mission of love in rescuing children in Africa. From his difficult beginnings as an abandoned child to becoming successful in business, Charles Mulli describes how God used these circumstances to shape him for his eventual role of being a father to so many fatherless children. He explains how, when circumstances seemed hopeless, he trusted in God. I have personally been amazed at his life. In spite of all the many great accomplishments, his life is one of simple and profound surrender to and reliance on Jesus. And it is this love for Jesus that impacts everything he does. In this book, Charles Mulli shows us that a life of faith is not just for a simple few. Rather, it is accessible to us all. Each of us wants our life to count. And Charles Mulli points us to how that is possible through a relationship with Christ.

Paul H. Boge
author of Father to the Fatherless: The Charles Mulli Story,
Hope for the Hopeless: The Charles Mulli Mission,
and The Biggest Family in the World

DR. CHARLES MUTUA MULLI
FOREWORD BY DR. CHARLES PRICE

My Journey
OF FAITH

AN ENCOUNTER WITH CHRIST
... and how He used me to spread His love to the poor

CASTLE QUAY BOOKS
WWW.CASTLEQUAYBOOKS.COM

MY JOURNEY OF FAITH: AN ENCOUNTER WITH CHRIST
AND HOW HE USED ME TO SPREAD HIS LOVE TO THE POOR

Copyright © 2016 Charles Mutua Mulli
All rights reserved
Printed in Canada
International Standard Book Number: 978-1-927355-77-0
ISBN 978-1-927355-78-7 EPUB

Published by:
Castle Quay Books
19-24 Laguna Pkwy, Lagoon City, Brechin, Ontario, L0K 1B0
Tel: (416) 573-3249
E-mail: info@castlequaybooks.com   www.castlequaybooks.com

Edited by Marina Hofman Willard and Paul Boge
Proofread by Lori Mackay
Cover design by Burst Impressions
Printed at Essence Printing, Belleville, Ontario

Library and Archives Canada Cataloguing in Publication

Mulli, Charles, author
    My journey of faith : an encounter with Christ ... and how he
used me to spread his love to the poor / Dr. Charles Mutua Mulli.
ISBN 978-1-927355-77-0 (paperback)

    1. Mulli, Charles. 2. Mully Children's Family--Biography.
3. Christian biography--Kenya. 4. Kenya--Biography. I. Title.

HV28.M84A3 2016   362.73'2096762   C2016-900169-5

CASTLE QUAY BOOKS
WWW.CASTLEQUAYBOOKS.COM

TABLE OF CONTENTS

FOREWORD

There is only one valid explanation for a true work of God—it is that God Himself is its source and its strength. Paul wrote in Romans 15:18, "I will not venture to speak of anything except what Christ has accomplished through me." That is the only story worth telling, and this is one such story you hold in your hand. It is an unfinished story of what Christ is accomplishing in that beautiful land of Kenya and in the broken lives of some of its people.

Not many parents can lay claim to having 2,500 children, but such is the relationship of Charles and Esther Mulli to their adopted family that each child knows them as "Mummy" and "Daddy." From the very small beginning of taking three young, helpless street children into their home to live alongside their biological family, Charles and Esther have become established as parents (as some have said) of the largest family in the world! But it's not just that they provide a roof over their heads and food in their stomachs, but a whole enterprise of education, health care, the development of barren land, business, a model of agriculture to the wider community and so much more has come about. Every sphere of life is included.

Of course there are human elements in this story. Charles Mulli himself had become a wealthy Kenyan businessman, despite the poverty and lack of opportunity of his own childhood. He laid aside all the benefits of material prosperity to invest in those who had nothing. But this alone does not suffice as an explanation! It is a story of the living God, taking possession of a humble family and enabling a stream of life to flow out of their hearts to bless and enrich others.

This work did not grow out of vision but out of opportunity. Every true work of God starts that way. As one opportunity is taken, another presents itself, ever growing, ever expanding, until a pattern and picture become clear about the way ahead. Part of that picture is unfinished. A university is now planned to provide a level of education and qualification for those unable to afford the normal means. And what next? Only God, in whose heart this began, really knows!

Enjoy this book, enjoy this family, and enjoy the God who is making it all happen.

Charles Price
former senior pastor of People's Church in Toronto, Canada
and host of Living Truth,
an hour-long international television ministry program

INTRODUCTION

Each of us is on a journey through life. We have the opportunity to choose the direction our life on earth will take. In my life, at a time when everything seemed completely hopeless, I responded to God's call and surrendered my life to Jesus Christ. That simple, profound act set my life on a journey of faith in rescuing thousands of children through Mully Children's Family (MCF) in Africa. I have experienced the transforming power of God's love in my own life and in the lives of many others. I have faced so many challenges and seen the impossible become possible. And I have encountered God every step of the way.

And this is possible for you, too.

My dream in writing this book is for you to gain a deeper understanding of our God who lives in us who believe—that you will have confidence in His power. I want to share my journey of faith with you so that you can have a glimpse of life up in the mountains and down in the valleys as I have overcome many challenges and done great things in the Lord. I hope this story will help you see how God is at work using His people today like He used them many years ago—people like Moses and Joshua.

And I hope this book will challenge you to evaluate yourself to see if you are living in the fulfillment of God's wonderful purpose for your life.

Be blessed and encouraged in the love of Jesus.

Charles Mutua Mulli

Chapter One

THE 25TH ANNIVERSARY

A Celebration of What God Has Accomplished

The MCF celebrated 25 years of existence on November 14, 2014. Within this period, we have been able—by the grace of God—to transform the lives of thousands of young Kenyan children and restore their hope after they had been abandoned. With the motto of "Saving Children's Lives" MCF has endeavoured to heal hurting souls and turn sad faces into happy ones. We have touched the lives of children who had no hope and have given them an opportunity to flourish.

These were 25 years of tremendous humanitarian intervention and transformation undertaken by MCF—a charitable organization that I established in 1989 to care for orphaned, vulnerable, abandoned, abused and neglected children.

It started with a simple, absolute surrender to God's call. And He has blessed it beyond what I could ever have imagined. We have major centres in Ndalani and Yatta in Machakos County and branches in Kitale (Kipsongo), Kilifi (Vipingo) and Lodwar. By the grace of God we have been used to rescue more than 10,000 precious children.

Friends, supporters, partners and other stakeholders from all over the world attended our silver jubilee celebration. We had guests from Uganda, Tanzania, Canada, Australia, Germany, America, Taiwan and other countries where we have friends who have partnered with us over the years to save children's lives. Over 3,000 people were in attendance. It was also a moment of reunion for MCF beneficiaries. Former MCF children who were serving in various capacities in Kenya and even globally were happy to come back home and meet with their daddy, mummy, brothers and sisters. The highly publicized event was covered live on national television.

The celebration took place at MCF Yatta and was marked by jubilation and thanksgiving as the children who were once desperate were now full of hope. Many of them had achieved their life dreams. Their beaming faces reflected a great sense of renewal, confidence and optimism. People who were once considered a nuisance were now very useful members of society. Most of them were already serving in key professions across the country and abroad. They gave moving testimonies of how MCF had positively impacted their lives.

Their stories of triumph filled my heart with joy. I was impressed and humbled to see how God had enabled us to go out and touch children's lives by turning their misery into victory. MCF has saved these thousands of children from the harsh, cruel street life and nurtured them into men and women of substance.

"I came here after being rescued from the streets, where I had lived for many years. I was so hopeless. But later I learned that it does not matter where you come from; what matters is where you are going," one of the beneficiaries testified. These sentiments were echoed by many other MCF beneficiaries.

It was amazing to hear the stories of children who used to rummage through garbage cans in the streets, for as many as ten years, who had never gone to school, had nothing to eat, had nowhere to sleep and did not know God. But all these circumstances changed. They came to know God and received an education, followed by special training for various careers. Now they are earning incomes and leading honourable lives.

These are children who used to spend their lives walking the streets, carrying heavy sacks filled with leftovers and satisfying their addiction to glue. Their health was poor due to persistent drug abuse, malnourishment and a diet consisting of mainly filthy leftovers found in the garbage. They did not know values such as honesty, courtesy, love or kindness. All they knew was fighting, abusing one another, plotting malice against one another, stealing and even killing.

But after undergoing rehabilitation at MCF, their lives changed dramatically for the better. They became physically, mentally, socially, emotionally and spiritually healthy. They came to lead dignified lives full of hope. Most of them have gone on to succeed in life.

They gave numerous testimonies about everything being possible with God. Their faces denoted happiness and contentment—something that told a very long and exciting story. This reinforced our theme for the day: *Celebrating 25 years of our unfathomable God.* It is true—God is unfathomable, because He can perform miracles that no human being understands. He can move mountains, He can change the course of a river, and He can make a way where there seems to be no way.

In Psalm 118:22, the Bible says, "The stone the builders rejected has become the cornerstone." This was true in the lives of these children. These children were the stone that was rejected. Just like in the story of the stone that was rejected by the builders, these children were considered less important in society. I personally witnessed how society regarded the children as less significant, but God transformed them into pillars of society. How is it possible that a child who had been in the streets for as many as ten years could eventually rise up to become a medical doctor? How could you expect an abandoned child from a remote cattle-rustling-prone area to defeat all odds to become a leading information technology expert with a global institution? Or how about the case of a former street child who eventually opens a children's home to rescue the helpless in society? Only God can make that possible.

Truly, it was difficult to understand and explain how God had touched and transformed the lives of these abandoned street children—who were rejected and written off everywhere they went—and turned them into doctors, engineers, teachers, accountants, managers and successful businesspeople, among other careers.

As we marked 25 years, we celebrated all the needy children who had already benefited directly from this charitable organization. Those who had benefited indirectly are triple that number. Another 2,500 were receiving various forms of assistance, mainly through formal education, vocational training, the provision of basic needs (food, clothing and shelter), mentorship and rehabilitation, among other forms of life support. As I quietly reflected over these statistics, it dawned on me that MCF had actually operated for many years and had accomplished a lot in society. I realized that we had come a long way and had accomplished many good things. Still, I felt we could go further.

Even as the beneficiaries, staff, friends and other stakeholders celebrated MCF's milestone, I sighed with relief, coupled with absolute astonishment, and thanked the Almighty God for having brought us this far. I knew that nothing happens without God's divine intervention and all that we had witnessed at MCF was a result of His mercy upon us. In the process, I remembered my favourite song:

This is the day that the Lord has made.
We will rejoice and be glad in it.
This is the day,
This the day that the Lord has made.

This was truly a special day that the Lord had made. It was a day that signified God's massive presence in MCF. I realized that our efforts to save children's lives had not been in vain. God's blessing upon MCF was abundant in the manner that the Bible says in Luke 6:38: "a good measure, pressed down, shaken together and running over."

Seeing representatives of the thousands of children who passed through MCF really touched me. I thanked God for giving me the energy and inspiration to serve and motivate these children, who all called me Daddy, and reflected on the role God placed me in. I came to realize that, beyond the usual roles of provider, caregiver, confidant and family peacekeeper, being a father means that you are a role model to your children. They will follow your steps, consider your opinions and learn from your example. Through this, I became more careful about the way I conducted myself, because they would adopt the behaviour that I portrayed. I realized that children learn more through observation than from what they are told. Thus I chose to be a good example—through actions—to help them prepare for a better tomorrow.

I resolved that as a father to thousands of children, I must make every effort to do the right thing at the right time and to make intelligent and thoughtful decisions that would benefit all the children under my care. I also learned to be a good listener, to be compassionate and patient. Furthermore, I purposed to be respectful and instill the same virtues in my thousands of children.

As the head of what is considered to be one of the largest families in the world, with over 2,500 children presently under care, not to mention those who have come and gone, I love each of my children, and I try to spend as much time with them as I can. I always create an opportunity to meet them regularly, both formally and informally, in their dormitories, in class, on the pitch, as they eat and when they walk in the compound. We crack jokes and bond while at the same time I listen to any issues that they have.

I spend most of my time with them encouraging them to be positive in life—to avoid looking at what they do not have and instead to learn to appreciate how far God had already brought them. As such, whenever we meet, we discuss matters pertaining to their future plans and aspirations.

All the same, I appreciate that in every home, especially a big one like MCF, there are a number of setbacks and challenges. But we purpose to treat them as minor hiccups and not permanent obstacles. I tell my children that challenges are only meant to test their resilience and not to deter them from marching on to victory. Furthermore, I encourage the children not to mourn over their past misfortunes but to focus on rebuilding their lives for future greatness.

Most importantly, I never discriminate against any of them, and this makes them grow up feeling they are part of a big, loving and caring family. I show them that they are not in MCF by accident but rather by the will of God. They belong here. They are part of this huge family.

I am always fully aware of the fact that most of the children we take into MCF have faced very difficult pasts. They have been rejected by their own family members and society. They have been discriminated against and treated as insignificant. People who were supposed to protect them abused them. And they have been molested and shown all manner of brutality and many other unfortunate happenings. Thus we strive to make a change and to show these children that they have invaluable worth and that we care for and love them. We endeavour to show them the other, good side of the world, which God desires for us all. That is when the true meaning of healing hurting souls is portrayed.

As we celebrated the silver jubilee, I recognized that the journey had not always been smooth. The MCF story has occasionally been full of hills, potholes, sharp thorns and rough, slippery surfaces. But I thank God for making us strong and enabling us to move on successfully and achieve our goals. Despite the challenges we face at MCF, I am always encouraged by God's promises to King Solomon in 2 Chronicles 7:14. It says, "If my people, who are called by my name, will humble themselves and pray and seek my face and turn from their wicked ways, then I will hear from heaven, and I will forgive their sin and will heal their land."

I tell the children to observe this proclamation—humble themselves before the Lord, and He will save their lives. In my talks with MCF children and staff, I have always maintained that we must be humble and respectful to God and those around us. I have strongly spoken against pride, dishonesty, thanklessness and selfishness and urged MCF family members to always remain down to earth and put the wishes of others first. And I came to notice that whenever you put others first, God even puts you ahead of them. I can testify that through us serving others well, God has listened to our prayers and lifted us up.

MCF has gone through an epic journey, full of surprising revelations from God. The initial 25 years showed me that with God everything is possible and that He does not forsake His people as long as they have faith in Him, obey His commandments and live by His Word. While on this mission, I learned that God can manifest Himself in very many ways, through all manner of people and actions. You never know when He is going to bless you. You can never predict His next step. He makes things happen when you least expect them to happen. Every time we pray to Him, He answers our prayers. It may take a day, a week, a month, a year or even a decade, but He will respond positively.

One particular blessing we celebrated is God's consistent provision for our need for food. Since 1989, my main concern and prayer request has been to feed the numerous children I have taken in. While living on the streets, they languished in hunger, and I would not have wished to see them go through the same while at MCF. At one point, all the food in our stores was depleted and the money in the bank was finished, but I knew God would not forsake us. He has always come to our rescue at the hour we were most in need. He has always touched people's hearts to provide aid.

As MCF grew, we felt the need to engage extensively in agriculture to ensure sustainability. God has enabled us to be self-sustaining by blessing our land and making it very productive. We have been able to grow food in a semi-arid part of Kenya. We even export food and sell it to Western parts of the world. The MCF farm has constantly supplied tomatoes, French beans, onions, eggs and other farm produce to markets in Kenya and even globally.

We saw God's favour when we joined a list of selected farms in Kenya that were awarded the Global GAP (Good Agricultural Practices) certification, which enables us to export our produce to European markets and other parts of the world. This international body sets standards for the certification of agricultural products around the globe. They took us through a thorough inspection process at the Yatta and Ndalani farms and confirmed that our agricultural practices met international standards and that our products were safe for consumption in international markets. As a result, we export French beans and tomatoes to European markets every week. The proceeds from these sales have been instrumental in feeding, educating and clothing our MCF children.

In Psalm 23:1 the Bible says, "The LORD is my shepherd, I lack nothing." This popular statement may sound quite familiar and ordinary, owing to its wide usage, but truly when you trust in God, you cannot lack anything, and neither can you fail to achieve the desires of your heart. MCF is a living testimony to this declaration.

We have seen God shepherd us compassionately. Despite the difficult times we have encountered, we have not lacked food for our children or the resources to educate them. Despite the harsh economic conditions in Kenya, we have been able to meet all our financial obligations. This truly manifested God's promise in Jeremiah 29:11: "For I know the plans I have for you...plans to prosper you and not to harm you, plans to give you hope and a future." This has come to pass. Though many children were leading hopeless lives in the streets, while others were orphaned and abandoned, God's plan was not to destroy them but rather to give them a hope and a future through MCF. I am glad that God chose to use MCF to fulfill one of His greatest promises to humankind.

In my child rescue mission, I have been strongly inspired by God's words in Genesis 50:19–21, which says, "But Joseph said to them, 'Don't be afraid. Am I in the place of God? You intended to harm me, but God intended it for good to accomplish what is now being done, the saving of many lives. So then, don't be afraid. I will provide for you and your children.'" Through His Word, I have learned not to be scared or afraid of anything. I have learned to trust in Him because He is a giver and saviour of lives. Through the example of Joseph in these verses, God manifested His love for humankind.

This explains why our success story at MCF has hinged on giving and doing something with all our heart without doubt, hesitation or complaining. It is important that when you do something, you do it with all your heart and with love. We should love others as if our lives depended on it. We should love like we may never love again, and we should always be ready to help and comfort the needy at all times. Be quick to give a meal to the hungry and a bed to the homeless. Be quick to show love to desperate and hurting souls. Be generous with the different things that God has given you. That way, God's cheerful presence will be evident in you.

This is summed up in 1 Peter 4:9–11:

> Offer hospitality to one another without grumbling. Each of you should use whatever gift you have received to serve others, as faithful stewards of God's grace in its various forms. If anyone speaks, they should do so as one who speaks the very words of God. If anyone serves, they should do so with the strength God provides, so that in all things God may be praised through Jesus Christ. To him be the glory and the power for ever and ever.

Furthermore, the Bible says in Deuteronomy 28:8–12,

> The LORD will send a blessing on your barns and on everything you put your hand to...The LORD will open the heavens, the storehouse of his bounty, to send rain on your land in season and to bless all the work of your hands. You will lend to many nations but will borrow from none.

These are some of the great Bible verses that have guided me since I embarked on helping the needy and vulnerable children in Kenya and across East Africa. Having witnessed the great power of God, I chose to be a man of deep faith. When others were full of worries and on the verge of giving up, I trusted in God to provide for all our needs.

Despite being located in a semi-arid region, MCF is one of the leading agricultural centres in Kenya. God has blessed the work of our hands, and we have been able to grow a lot of food to feed our children, sell some of it for sustainability, and share the rest with the hungry community. We receive hardly any meaningful rainfall throughout the year, the temperatures are usually high, and yet we are able to irrigate our farms to yield a significant produce. We grow maize, tomatoes and French beans among other farm produce for the sustainability of the centre. Our barns are full of harvests, and our children have never lacked food. This is a manifestation of God's love for His people.

Finally, our anniversary celebration was a testimony of the joy that God has brought to everyone at MCF for 25 years. The Lord has gifted the MCF children with the exceptional blessing of being able to smile and play regardless of all the misfortunes they faced earlier in life. I often listen to the sounds of joy that come from the children at MCF. I hear nothing that mirrors the horrifying past that they endured. Despite being orphaned, abandoned or abused before being rescued by MCF, these children are now some of the happiest people in Kenya. They talk with each other, crack jokes and are full of happiness. The levels of love and interaction are encouraging.

Through our guidance the MCF children have learned to take life as it comes and are only focused on creating a better future for themselves. This is a result of constantly encouraging them to forget the past and walk with Jesus Christ into the future. I often tell them that if they focus on their past misfortunes they will only end up pitying themselves and will eventually miss seeing the good things God has planned for them.

But, as they fix their eyes on Jesus, the author and perfecter of their faith, they are transformed with a genuine and true radiance. They become the people they were designed to be. And it is the immense joy experienced by my children that has formed the basis of my happiness as I help them rebuild their lives.

Since I embarked on this ministry in 1989 my life has totally changed. I am happier than I used to be. I get more excited, especially when I see a child who was once abandoned in the streets, left for dead, rejected and even abused, but who is now able to run around joyfully, feeling part of a loving family, pursuing education and being able to achieve his or her dreams without limitations or segregation.

Furthermore, I get a lot of joy from seeing MCF children surrender their lives to Christ and embrace His righteousness. This restoration of souls for Christ gives me extreme joy.

Happiness is the greatest blessing that God has given to the children of MCF, and that's what we endeavour to sustain. The truth of this blessing made a strong impact on me in July 2013 when I listened to a very emotional testimony from a medical doctor who decided to help us.

This doctor came to us with a team of professionals and other volunteers. The team set up a free medical camp in MCF Ndalani to attend various patients, especially those from the community around MCF who were unable to access medical care. This doctor struggled with the realization that he was coming to meet and help needy and suffering children in Africa. He had never been to Africa before. But he had heard of it as a place full of suffering and sadness. And so he had prepared himself to offer both medical and, as a counsellor on family matters, psychosocial services.

The doctor admitted to me that before he boarded the plane to Nairobi, he had in his mind a picture of suffering, crying, sad and very sick people who needed a lot of material and moral support. He came to Kenya thinking that he was going to meet a very dejected and suffering population.

But when he arrived in Ndalani, he was surprised that the so-called needy and suffering children were instead very happy, making a lot of noise while playing with each other in the field and running all over the compound. These children lined up to sing and welcome the Canadian team. And when the children went for devotional services, they sang melodious songs and danced with joy.

The doctor did not meet depressed and miserable faces as he had expected. He was taken aback. He wondered how children with a sad past, no parents, no proper clothing and no shoes were able to be so happy. He even contrasted the MCF scenario with the well-to-do society of the Western world where he said children were given virtually every material thing that they desired in life—good shoes, food, cars, housing, a good education, luxurious holidays—but they were habitually unhappy. He said that as a psychologist and motivational speaker, this scenario had been bothering him for many years.

He revealed to me as we chatted outside the MCF Ndalani Medical Clinic, "I thought I was coming here to help alleviate the suffering of these children and other community members, but I have instead ended up being helped by them. I have realized that happiness has nothing to do with material possessions. It has nothing to do with social class. It's all about accepting God and allowing Him to dwell in you in spite of the circumstances you are in. I now know that one can be happy, regardless of what they own or do not own."

The doctor and the other volunteers, in conjunction with the MCF medical team, helped to treat hundreds of Yatta sub-county residents. The 10-day exercise took place from July 2 to 12, 2014. It saw over 2,000 people from the Ndalani, Yatta, Kithimani, Sofia and Matuu areas given specialized diagnoses and the treatment of various ailments such as malaria, typhoid, fever, body pains, common cold and arthritic related complications, among other diseases. Specialist doctors were also on hand to handle issues related to dental and eye problems.

Their team leader, Annie, said they were in Kenya to use their medical skills to give back to the society. She said, "We thank God for the various skills and knowledge that He has given us, and we want to be useful to the suffering people of God."

All of this caused me to reflect on what God has accomplished in my life. As a child, I would never have predicted my life would have turned out the way it has. Who could possibly have imagined that all this could happen? And yet, when I think of the greatness of God—how awesome, powerful and loving He is—I see how His faithfulness has made everything possible.

Chapter Two

HUMBLE BEGINNINGS

It is amazing to realize all that God has accomplished in my life from where I began. It reminds me that God is never limited by our circumstances.

I was born on January 7, 1949, in Kathithyamaa village in Kangundo, Machakos County. I am the firstborn among ten children, nine boys and one girl. Our childhood was very difficult because our poor parents could hardly provide for us.

We lived from hand to mouth, one day at a time. My father, Daudi Kaleli, was a squatter with no land of his own. He occasionally worked on farms with my mother, Rhoda Mukina, in order to feed us. In most cases, whenever they could not provide for us, we had to seek other means of survival for ourselves elsewhere.

In an attempt to cope with our difficult life, my father would often stay away from home. He would only come back at night, and often very drunk. He developed violent tendencies, which added more domestic problems to the already existing ones.

Our clothing was nothing more than tatters. Our housing was ramshackle. I led the life of a street child. The only difference between me and the present-day street children is that I never roamed around in town streets or sniffed glue. Still, I had many similarities with them. I regularly begged for food from neighbours and wandered a lot in the village, to the point that I became a nuisance. Some children from well-to-do families laughed at me as I asked for something to eat from their parents. It was humiliating. But I chose to be ashamed and embarrassed rather than to die of hunger.

When I was six years old, my parents left for Molo in the then Rift Valley province to search for employment. They hoped to earn a living by doing menial jobs in the expansive agricultural farms. I was left in the care of an aunt, who was also very poor. Together with my siblings, I led a life of begging for food from neighbours and other well-wishers. It was not an easy thing to do. But the survival instinct has a strange way of helping to overcome feelings of shame. I regularly moved from one relative to another seeking help, just trying to hang on in life, doing nothing more than existing.

My day started with standing under a scorching sun. I would eat sugarless porridge on those rare occasions when we were able to have something to eat. I would then plot my next move to find some manual job to do in the village. Some days we found work and eventually got some food. But often there were no jobs. And that meant no food.

Despite the harsh economic and social challenges that surrounded us, I had a burning ambition and desire to succeed and make a difference in my life and the lives of my family members. So I tracked the whereabouts of my parents to the city of Molo, where my father was working in white colonial settler farms. Here I started class (grade) 1. But life continued to be unbearable. Not only did we not have food or clothing, my drunken father had sunk even deeper into alcoholism.

I returned to Kangundo a year later and joined the Kyamulendu primary school. I later transferred to Kathithyamaa, where I lived with my relatives. By the grace of God, I was able to complete primary education (grade 8) in 1966 at the age of 17. Unfortunately, I never proceeded to secondary school, due to a lack of money for the fees.

With so many struggles, I began to lose hope in life. I felt that my fate on earth had been sealed—that I was bound to suffer throughout my entire life. I developed a feeling that I would never progress in life. I saw myself as doomed.

I even contemplated committing suicide.

But little did I know that God had good plans for me. He had a purpose for my life. He had designed me to carry out a specific calling.

Yet all of this would happen only in His perfect timing.

During that period of suffering and confusion, a friend invited me to a church event taking place in the nearby town of Kangundo. I decided to go, even though I was not born again and had little interest in the Word of God. I was raised in a society where the Bible was hardly ever mentioned. God was not on my mind. However, I chose to attend this event out of curiosity to see how Christians did their singing and dancing.

When I arrived at the church, I saw a huge crowd. As the pastor preached, I felt he was talking about the very things that were happening in my life. He talked about Christ's invitation to those who were carrying heavy burdens in their hearts to come to Him and find rest. He talked about God being able to create a way where there seems to be no way and that He turns around difficult circumstances.

"Come to Him, those who labour, and He will comfort you," the preacher said. "Cast your burden unto Jesus, because He cares for you," the pastor went on to beseech the gathering. He then added, "For God so loved the world that He gave His only begotten Son, that whoever believes in Him shall not perish, but have eternal life." He summed up by reading a Scripture that said, "I am the way and the truth, and the life. No one comes to the Father except through me" (John 14:6). I felt the fire of salvation burning within me, and without hesitation I gave my life to Christ that day. I became a born-again Christian. I found a new bearing in life and a renewed hope in God. I was able to relax and allow God to take control of my life.

I went back home a very happy and relieved young man. I had been battling with so many needs, worrying about many things in life—poverty, a lack of education and a bleak future. The more I worried about them, the more difficult they became. I now resolved to allow God to take control of my life and carry my burden. I acquired a small New Testament Bible, which I carried with me in my pocket wherever I went. I mandated myself to read it at least once a day.

As I read the Bible and committed myself to God, I was impacted by 1 Peter 5:5–11:

> You who are younger, submit yourselves to your elders. All of you, clothe yourselves with humility toward one another, because, "God opposes the proud but shows favor to the humble." Humble yourselves, therefore, under God's mighty hand, that he may lift you up in due time. Cast all your anxiety on him because he cares for you. Be alert and of sober mind. Your enemy the devil prowls around like a roaring lion looking for someone to devour. Resist him, standing firm in the faith, because you know that the family of believers throughout the world is undergoing the same kind of sufferings. And the God of all grace, who called you to his eternal glory in Christ, after you have suffered a little while, will himself restore you and make you strong, firm and steadfast. To him be the power for ever and ever. Amen.

Yes, "Cast all your anxiety on him because he cares for you." As a young person, I felt that this section of the Bible was directly addressing me. I chose to obey it fully. Prior to the Kangundo gospel event, I had become desperate. I had thought that taking my own life was the only way out. I saw nothing good in life. But this portion of Scripture reminded me that God cares for me.

At that moment, I was weak both physically and emotionally because I lacked most of the things I desired in life. Yet this verse revealed to me that the "God of all grace, who called you to his eternal glory in Christ, after you have suffered a little while, will himself restore you and make you strong."

One day, on a visit to my relatives in Kithimani, I received information that the government was recruiting soldiers for the Kenya Army. There were only two days to go before the exercise would take place in Machakos. I had been harbouring a desire to join the military because I thought I was strong and capable of serving in the disciplined forces. Whenever I encountered soldiers, I would look at them in awe and admiration. So now I had to move quickly in order to try my luck at getting enlisted.

Because of my lack of resources, I did not have even a shilling to board a vehicle to Machakos. My relatives in Kithimani could not help either. But this did not deter me from going to Machakos to attend the recruitment exercise. By faith, I decided to walk all the way from Kithimani to Machakos town through the expansive Yatta plateau. This would be a 50-kilometre journey. I left home very early and walked through thickets, rocks and grasslands under the scorching sun of Ukambani.

There was no specific road to follow. I got my bearings through natural geography as I walked towards Machakos to secure my goal of a military job. At times I would walk for over five kilometres without seeing a home or even meeting a single person. Whenever I met people on the road, I asked them for the directions. I was glad when their answers indicated I was heading in the right direction.

I was alone for most of the journey. I feared being attacked by wild animals, but that did not deter me from soldiering on. I only stopped occasionally to eat wild fruit and drink water from the river. During this journey I was convinced that "though I walk through the valley of death, I will fear no evil, because the Lord protects me."

Between the towns of Kithimani and Machakos, I had to cross two major rivers, the Athi River and the Thwake River. I managed to cross the Athi River with the help of young men who had boats. Their work was to help people cross from one side to the other for a fee of 50 cents. I used my last coin to pay for their service.

Nightfall found me in Kabaa, and I slept in the corner of one of the shops. I resumed my journey early the following morning and walked straight into the Iveti hills; I did not go in the Makutano direction. Scaling these hills was not easy, but I managed to climb up and descend down the rocks.

When I came to the Thwake River, there was no bridge to cross over. But as a determined young man nothing was going to hinder me from reaching my desired destination. I waded through the waters and managed to cross the river by the use of sticks to measure the depth and employing the hop, step and jump style, also known as triple jump. I arrived in Machakos town just as the evening was approaching, very tired and very hungry.

I did not know anyone in Machakos town. I did not have any money for food or accommodation. Strangely, after such a long and difficult journey, I felt neither hungry nor tired. All I longed for was to join the army and get an opportunity to turn my life around. I spotted some young men talking by the roadside, and I humbly approached them, greeted them and told them that I had come all the way from Kithimani to attend a military recruitment exercise. I asked them to show me where the recruitment would take place so that I could go and stay there in readiness for the event. I had planned to sleep on the verandah or in the corridors of the recruitment venue.

One of the young men told me that he also had intentions of joining the military and was going to present himself for recruitment. "I'm aware of the army selections, and I will be going there to try my luck. I really want to be a soldier," he said. I looked at his body frame, and in my assessment he was fit for the job. He warmed up to me, asked me about Kithimani, and even offered to host me in his home so that we could go together in the morning for the selections. He was a godsend. Those were the days when people were never scared of strangers. Those were the days when honesty, generosity, kindness and brother-hood, among other good virtues, were highly regarded. We knew that everybody meant well for one another. That evening I was able to eat and sleep well in a stranger's house.

Through this experience, I gathered that God has His own way of preserving His people. He always sends someone ahead of you. He creates a road where there is none. He protects you from evil. And He provides for you.

The following day we left early in the morning and walked about five kilometres from my host's home to the Machakos stadium. We were among the first to arrive. Our first test was a simple drill—the recruitment team wanted to assess our strength through a running exercise. We were told to run about 10 times around the stadium. I was a good athlete and managed to finish among the first group. Over 200 people had turned up for the exercise, but close to half were dismissed right away for either finishing late or not being able to complete the race. According to those recruiting, the good runners already had one foot in the military.

When one was told "go to the right," he was moved on to the next level. Those who were told "go to the left" had failed the test. That was an automatic disqualification with no chance for appeal. Everyone's prayer was to hear "go to the right."

After the running exercise I was told "go to the right." I was happy about my performance so far. My hope of joining the military was beginning to be realized.

The next test was an assessment of our body, height and general fitness. The recruitment team also checked for any sign of physical deformity. When they examined my body frame from top to bottom, everything was well: my height was desirable, as I was above five feet tall; I had no problem with my eyes; my teeth were white and none of them was missing; my hands were straight; there were no missing fingers; my legs were straight; and I walked upright. So far, so good. I had met the conditions for joining the military.

I was waiting to be told "go to the right." But one military man re-examined me and asked, "What happened to your leg here?" He pointed to a white scar on my left leg. It was an injury that I sustained over 10 years earlier when I was cooking porridge for my siblings. The serving spoon toppled over and landed on my leg, scalding me with boiling porridge. I was severely injured and could not walk for months. I was never taken to hospital. There was no money for treatment. The injury grew worse and even started emitting a foul smell. My leg became terribly swollen. With no medical attention, it took over six months for the wound to heal, and I was left with a permanent scar on my leg. This military man noticed. He looked me straight in the eyes, paused for a moment, and said, "Go to the left."

Just like that, I had missed the chance. I felt so disappointed. But I knew that there was a reason for everything. The exercise was conducted in a quick manner and left no room for negotiations or appeal. If you were ordered to leave, you had to depart immediately. I left the Machakos stadium a very downtrodden man. But I asked God to preserve me so that I could fight another day.

I went back to my relatives in Kithimani on foot, just as I had left. While there, I worked on a coffee plantation and other farms for about a month. My work was to clear the weeds and prune the coffee plants. I also engaged in picking coffee and transporting it to the nearby factory. However, this job ended, and I returned to my home in Kangundo to search for other ways of earning a living. I did not wish to stay at home and pity myself, so I kept trying out different avenues to earn income.

But while at home, things kept going from bad to worse. We would go for days without food. We only survived by begging from neighbours, which had become our normal routine. There was nothing to do to earn a living; even the common manual jobs like weeding, harvesting and transporting farm produce to the market were not easy to come by. I longed to get a job of digging in someone's farm in Kangundo, but I was never hired. Eventually, I considered relocating to a town where opportunities were unlimited, maybe Machakos or even Nairobi.

One evening, I sat quietly and prayed to God to take charge of my life. I asked Him not to forsake me in my hour of need. I told God that I was relying on Him totally to make a change in my life. After a long period of meditation and prayer, I went to sleep.

I woke up the following morning feeling quite energetic, and I made an instant decision to leave home and go to Nairobi to look for employment. The epic and risky journey to Nairobi, 70 kilometres away, saw me pass through thickets and bare land. It took me three days to reach the city. Despite numerous dangers on the way, I remained determined as I walked in faith.

This happened barely three years after Kenya had attained independence. The government's agenda was to develop its citizens and give them jobs, land and business opportunities for national growth. Children who had performed well in their exams were being given scholarships to study abroad. Those were the days when people with various desirable academic qualifications were taken from their homes to go and serve in government offices, schools, industries, corporate organizations and other places.

Having stopped schooling in class 8, I did not possess meaningful academic papers (certificate, diploma or degree) that could help me secure a white collar job. Even though the white collar jobs were not as limited in those days as they are now, I knew I stood no chance of serving in an office. The realistic option for me was to use my hands and other relevant life skills to eke out a living. I was ready to do any kind of job. I had done a lot of farm work at home, and I did not mind doing more as long as it would enable me to generate income and stop me from having to beg from people.

I arrived in Nairobi and came face-to-face with a huge city full of people. I did not know anybody here. I could not even figure out my way around the many streets. There were many people rushing about, everyone minding their own business, not talking to each other. This was not what I was used to back in my village. Nobody greeted me in Nairobi. I would have received many greetings in Kangundo.

I walked through the streets, admiring the levels of development. The buildings were big and clean. The roads were good. Everything looked smart. The people were well dressed. The items on display in the shops were marvellous. There were so many people in town. But I also noticed a couple of beggars and street families.

After walking aimlessly through the city, I became very hungry. I had not tasted a meal since I left Kangundo three days previously. I had been surviving on only water and wild fruits. I slept on the town pavement for another two nights. On the third day, I walked outside the city and found myself in one of the high-end estates. It was mainly inhabited by Europeans and Asians. It had nice bungalows. The compounds were full of trees and well-manicured lawns. The gates were large and made of iron. Years later, I learned that this was the Runda estate.

I knocked on one of the gates repeatedly until an Asian woman came out. She was visibly angry. "Why are you disturbing us?" she asked me. I told her that I was desperate and I wanted some food to eat. She hesitated for a moment and then told me, "Come inside." She gave me some very good food, and I gulped it down quickly.

I thanked her profusely for her kind gesture. I then told her I was looking for a job. "I will do any job you want," I told her.

She did not mull it over for long. She called one of the senior workers, who came running, and instructed him to assign me duties in the garden.

I became engaged in tilling the garden, cutting grass, pruning flowers, washing clothes and cooking in the kitchen, among other domestic chores. My salary was 65 Kenyan shillings (KSh65) per month. This was good money at the time. I could afford to buy clothes and even had money for my mother and siblings.

Suddenly my life changed. It was now good. I did not worry about my next meal, because I was given three meals a day by my employer. Plus, I was given a room and a bed to sleep on. I repeatedly thanked God for creating this chance for me.

While doing this work, I exhibited a lot of patience, honesty, trustworthiness and commitment. Most importantly, I obeyed my employer. Every time I was assigned a duty I ensured that I accomplished it well. Generally, I liked doing my work with a degree of perfection. Whenever I cleaned the compound I ensured it was thorough. The same applied to washing utensils and even pruning flowers. Some of my fellow workers complained that the pay was so little; they felt like we were slaves who suffered as others enjoyed. But I had a different opinion. I told them I had come from a worse situation than this. So I had every reason to like my job and be happy.

Six months later, the man I was working for, Mr. De Souza, though I hardly interacted with him, decided to transfer me from his house in Nairobi to his company (Kakuzi Ltd.) in Thika, where he was the managing director. Initially I never knew where my employer worked. All I gathered was that he was a rich man who owned a palatial home in the city, drove a very nice car, bought so many things for his family, and occasionally held parties for his friends at his house.

So on that morning, on the day of transfer, I received a message that the boss wanted to see me. I was scared. Most people who received such messages ended up being sent away. Normally, when the boss summoned us, we rushed to clean our hands and feet before going to meet him. I quickly spruced myself up and rushed to the main house. I was told to dress well and wait at the gate.

When the tall man came out of the house, he called me to enter his Mercedes car. I could not believe what I was experiencing—a *shamba* boy being given a ride in his employer's luxurious car. We went for about one hour along the present Thika road, past Thika town, before reaching the Kakuzi farm, where he appointed me to serve as a farm clerk. This was a very huge promotion. I worked both in the office and on the farm. My duties included keeping a record of workers who had reported on duty. This farm had over 200 workers. My salary increased. Slowly but surely, my life was beginning to take a new turn. God had released His favour upon me.

Here I exhibited strong managerial and leadership skills and was further promoted to the position of an assistant manager. My job entailed assigning workers their duties in the farm and supervising the coffee picking process.

While working in Kakuzi I met and fell in love with Esther Nthenya, who was also a casual worker, and we eventually got married on December 22, 1970.

Then came another step forward. In 1971, I joined Strabag Road Construction Company in Mwea, Embu County, where I was put in charge of the stores. I was not given a specific title, but this position was similar to a procurement officer. I was involved in receiving construction materials from suppliers, storing them, issuing them to workers and keeping records.

Later that year, Strabag was awarded a tender to construct the Timboroa-Eldoret and Nyaru-Eldoret roads in the then Rift Valley Province. I was transferred to this region in the same capacity.

In 1972, the Strabag Company completed its road construction project in Kenya and embarked on a new project in Saudi Arabia. I was offered an opportunity to continue working with Strabag in the new location in the Middle East. But after a moment of soul-searching, I declined the offer and opted to remain in Nyaru, where I continued to engage in various business activities, mainly public transport.

I became a bona fide resident of Nyaru. This was a forested place with temperatures much colder than I was used to. The transport system was very poor. It was not easy to travel to Eldoret due to a lack of vehicles. Eventually I decided to start a *matatu* (taxi) business along the Eldoret-Nyaru route. I drove the vehicle myself. My business expanded, and I bought minibuses. I christened the company Mullyways, and it operated between Kapenguria, Eldoret, Nairobi and Machakos.

Besides the transport business, I operated a small shop in Nyaru that was managed by my wife, Esther. I also engaged in different agricultural ventures, which included dairy farming, poultry keeping and large-scale farming of maize in Uasin-Gishu for commercial purposes.

With time, my business ventures flourished, and I built a house in Pioneer Estate in the town of Eldoret, where I relocated with my family. I diversified further by opening a hardware shop and establishing Mullyways Agencies Ltd., a multi-purpose company that dealt in insurance, microfinance, real estate agency, security and debt collection. I even bought 50 acres of land on the Thika River in Ndalani that I would use a retirement property for our family.

Esther and I were blessed with seven children: Janey, Grace, Ndondo, Kaleli, Mueni, Isaac and Dickson. We also adopted and raised Miriam, my youngest sister. I enrolled them for school in the then prestigious Kaptagat Preparatory. As a devoted family man, I ensured that my children grew up to be responsible people. I led them in daily devotions where they sang and memorized Bible verses. Everything had exceeded my wildest expectations.

At least that's what I thought.

Chapter Three

A CALL TO RESPOND TO THE VOICE OF SUFFERING CHILDREN

The MCF journey started in Eldoret in 1989 when I received a calling from God to undertake a special duty for His people, the duty of help-ing the helpless in society and restoring hope among the hopeless chil-dren. In those early days, I had no idea of the magnitude of how this work could grow. I started out by simply trusting in God and believing that greater things could come.

Eldoret town, at that time, was full of street children, who were con-sidered a nuisance by the members of the public. These destitute chil-dren were all over the town streets, bus parks, market centres, dump-sites and even estates. Many people could not stand them. The children were dirty and uncultured. They were stinky and offensive. They were seen as bothersome beggars as they followed people with a persistent plea for money, saying, "Auntie, Uncle, *nisaidie shilingi,*" meaning, "Please spare me a shilling."

I heard street boys asking me for a shilling when I parked my car in Nairobi one day. They showed me to a parking spot and wanted me to reward them for their help, but I denied them any money. When I had finished my business meeting, I came out to discover my car had been stolen. This greatly impacted me. In fact, this one incident set in motion a chain of events and started a process where I became more and more convicted about the plight of street children.

But I did not immediately respond. Just like Samuel in the Bible, the little boy who lived in the priest Eli's household (1 Samuel 3) and later became a prophet, I too was called many times by the Lord but could not immediately grasp the message that He was communicating to me.

In the biblical story, God wants to use Samuel to guide the children of Israel. I could relate to Samuel. One night, the Lord calls the young boy Samuel.

> Samuel answered, "Here I am." And he ran to Eli and said, "Here I am; you called me." But Eli said, "I did not call; go back and lie down." So he went and lay down.
> Again the LORD called, "Samuel!" And Samuel got up and went to Eli and said, "Here I am; you called me."
> "My son," Eli said, "I did not call; go back and lie down." Now Samuel did not yet know the LORD: The word of the LORD had not yet been revealed to him. (1 Samuel 3:4–7)

Samuel must have been so confused!

> A third time the LORD called, "Samuel!" And Samuel got up and went to Eli and said, "Here I am; you called me." Then Eli realized that the LORD was calling the boy. So Eli told Samuel, "Go and lie down, and if he calls you, say, 'Speak, LORD, for your servant is listening.'" So Samuel went and lay down in his place.
> The LORD came and stood there, calling as at the other times, "Samuel! Samuel!" Then Samuel said, "Speak, for your servant is listening." (1 Samuel 3:8–10)

And the Lord went ahead and gave Samuel the intended message.

Many times I had felt a lot of compassion for street children, to the extent of taking food to them in the street, mainly bread and soda, chatting with them, encouraging them not to give up in life (however unbelievable such words sounded), but God had wanted me to do something bigger than that. During that time I kept asking myself, *What is the reason for our existence on earth?* I felt a compelling force pushing me to go forth and do something about these abandoned and vulnerable children. But what was I supposed to do?

I could not quickly figure it out. I spent sleepless nights pondering it. This was characterized by moments of prayer, meditation and soul-searching. I continued making trips to the streets of Eldoret, the place this vulnerable group called home. At one point I became a very troubled man—not happy or contented with what I was doing, despite succeeding in a lot of businesses and earning a lot of money.

I kept feeling that God was calling me to something different. I even felt guilty that I had a lot of food for myself and my family, but the street children were suffering out there with nothing to eat and no roof over their heads. For about three years, I kept getting signs from God, telling me, "Go ye, Charles," but it was not until November 1989 that I finally said, "Speak, Lord; your servant is listening."

The turning point came that November day when I suddenly became ill at my office. I left for home, yet strangely found myself on the highway headed to Uganda. I blacked out and nearly crashed. I pulled over and felt an incredible battle inside me. *Do I stay in business, or do I leave it all to rescue street children?* It was crazy, really. But there is nothing normal about following God.

After a moment of silent meditation and prayer, I realized that God wanted me to rescue and show love to the suffering children in the streets of Eldoret and the rest of the country. Most of them were totally hopeless and desperate; they had concluded that God had forgotten them. They believed that their lives were headed nowhere. But at this moment, God was calling me to show these children that He still cared about them and, despite being destitute in the streets, all was not lost in their lives.

And the message finally came out loud: "Go ye, Charles, into the streets and rescue the suffering children from the trauma that they are facing out there. Restore them back to Me. Give them food, clothing and shelter. Let them know Me and know that I love and care for them. Sell everything that you own and dedicate those resources to uplifting the lives of the destitute children."

Just like a soldier who had been commanded into action by his superiors, I sprang to my feet with my heart blazing. I focused all my energies on rescuing and rehabilitating the needy children by giving them food, clothing, shelter, spiritual guidance, parental love and education.

But before doing all this, I sought to know and understand the street children better. There was no better way of doing this than befriending them and going to the streets to spend time with them. I knew I had to befriend them and get to know their ways before I could teach them the ways of the Lord.

Most evenings I would go down to the banks of the Sosiani River in Eldoret—where they mainly lived—and try to understand their lives. What do they talk about? How do they reason? How do they connect? How do they eat? Where do they sleep? Whom do they worship? How do they perceive life? What do they hope for in the future? I decided to find out.

I sat around their fires and shared in their stories. Sosiani River cuts through Eldoret town. It often floods whenever it rains. This is a dirty and dangerous river, and many people drown in it. I could not understand why street children chose to live next to this dangerous place where it could be catastrophic if someone pushed you over the edge. My worries were compounded when I realized that some children liked pushing others in. All the same, I joined them there.

I learned that the children on the street barely ate anything. They went for days without food. And when they happened to eat something, it was mainly decomposing leftovers that exposed them to serious dangers like cancer and even death. They slept in the open alleys and literally saw nothing positive in the world.

These children became a bother to the public. They begged in streets and camped outside hotels and supermarkets, begging for assistance, but few people would give them a second glance.

It is not a secret that even today many people find these children repulsive and bothersome. Many people shout at them or simply roll up their car windows and drive off. This attitude leads some of the street children into stealing, but the consequences became even worse. Many of them were brutally attacked, injured and even killed. I witnessed and also heard of many cases of street children dying by the hands of irate citizens. It pitted a society of those who have against those who do not have.

The street children were commonly referred to as *chokora*. This name refers to people whose main preoccupation is to rummage in garbage cans and dumpsites. It is a negative term suggesting that the children are very disgusting, disorderly and unbearable. Instead of pitying and supporting the poor, it is sad that our society chose to look down upon them and coined a demeaning name for them.

I don't like using the word *chokora* in reference to street children. This term literally accuses them of being wild or vagabonds and portrays them in a negative light, whereas some of them are living in the streets as a matter of fate. Given a chance, they would not have gone there at all.

My interaction with street children revealed that most of them hardly knew where they came from. Some were dumped in the streets when they were barely two years old. They could not understand anything or even defend themselves. By the grace of God they managed to hang on to life, and the streets became their ultimate home. Others are in the streets as a result of having lost their parents and nobody else would come to their support. The streets became their last resort. Such children need to be understood and comforted, but not shouted at and called chokora.

Through interactions with street children, I learned that street life—just like in the jungle—was about survival of the fittest and preying on each other. It was full of selfishness, anger, disorder, hatred, fear, blackmail and undue opportunism, among other vices. The children struggled to get something to eat by any means possible, including stealing, lying, pretending and even concealing their identity. In this jungle—where their ages ranged from as young as 2 years old up to 25 years old—the strong ones had it all while the weakest were hit worst. Life was not so different from the animal kingdom, where the weak ate only after the strong had their fill. Woe unto the young ones, because the big ones hardly ever had their fill.

The girls in the streets were sexually abused by the big boys and even other members of the public. It was common to see small girls aged 12 years having babies or getting infected with HIV/AIDS. Most of the adult street boys and girls were already infected with HIV/AIDS. The situation was appalling. It signalled to me the need for urgent intervention.

Besides the prevalence of the deadly virus, the children were also used by criminal elements for illicit trade such as drug trafficking—and abused drugs themselves. Selling and smoking of marijuana (*bhang*) was common in the streets. The huge, dirty, black sacks that some of the children carried on their backs—that were mostly believed to contain food leftovers—also contained drugs. Sometimes I would talk to street children who were too intoxicated to see me. When we later met again, they had no idea who I was.

The jungle life was strongly exhibited when children struggled for food. If a small child, for instance, got a piece of bread and went with it to a given "camp" where other street kids lived, it would be grabbed from them mercilessly by the stronger ones and devoured as they watched. It was even worse if someone stumbled on food in the presence of others; they could fight for it and end up injuring one another badly. Every time I went to the camp in the evening, I would be told of cases where children quarrelled over food. Such living conditions left no room for love, courtesy, friendliness, orderliness, meekness, humility or concern for other people's welfare. It only created men and women full of selfishness, anger and vindictiveness, practising blackmail and other anti-social behaviours.

On almost any day, at almost any time, children dressed in rags with bottles filled with glue pressed to their faces roam the streets in Kenyan towns. Even today they can be seen, roaming in rural towns, too. Many have lost their parents to the deadly HIV/AIDS scourge and other diseases. Some have been cast out of their homes. Many are runaways, while most of the others are forced on the streets due to poverty. Remember, we have millions of Kenyans out there who live on less than half a dollar per day. These children are the poorest of the poor; they depend on begging, theft and prostitution to survive. Sniffing glue and smoking marijuana are also popular among these children.

I would spend time with my wife and children in the evening, talking to them about God and His love for the poor, sharing with them my desires for street children. We would have dinner together and pray together as a family. When they went to bed at around 9 p.m., I would go out to meet the street children. I would stay there in the dark up to 3 a.m. or sometimes until morning before driving back to my house in Pioneer Estate. My wife and children were worried about my security at night, but I told them, "I'm doing God's work, and He is watching over me."

Initially, the street children were suspicious of my intentions for visiting their riverside camp. Perhaps they thought I was a police officer or a security informer tracking their movements. Many of these children were involved in petty crimes and were repeatedly arrested and beaten by the police. The authorities simply called it discipline.

But with time the children relaxed and welcomed me into their open abode, especially after I kept taking food to them every evening. They were used to people abusing, beating and harassing them, but when they saw me coming with food they opened up and warmly received me. After walking aimlessly in the streets and rummaging through dumpsites during the day, these children would rush back to the riverbank in the evening to wait for me. They were sure I would come. They were sure I would bring food. They were sure they would eat. I became one of them. This gave me a chance to get to know them better.

My wife, Esther, would cook a lot of food and pack it in containers. I would deliver it to the children at night. Initially, the children fought over it, but I created order and supervised the sharing exercise. On other occasions, I bought them bread, soda and milk. This made them so happy, and they started longing for my arrival every evening. And while they ate the food, I taught them the art of sharing among themselves and appreciating one another. The rehabilitation process had started.

As my relationship with them became stronger they started telling me their stories. I even learned their language—the popular street *sheng*—which we used to communicate with each other. For instance, they would get excited when I greeted them with *"Ooooyeeee."* To them it was a moment of excitement, but for me it was a learning session. This expression would later become synonymous with MCF. In our interactions, the children frequently used words like *buda* (father), *msosi* (food), *niaje* (how are you?) and many other words that I have since forgotten. Today when I interact with the MCF children I still greet them with *"Ooooyeeee."* This phrase also means "Peace be with you."

While visiting the street children, I discovered that some were very sickly, especially the young ones who were less than 10 years old, because of the cold temperatures they were exposed to in the streets. In the months of June, July and August, it would get as low as 10 degrees Celsius (50 degrees Fahrenheit). These children had no choice but to brave the cold by the riverside or on wet pavements. Some of them would cry in my presence, cough endlessly and shiver throughout the night. Others had acute cases of fever and diarrhea. I took them to the hospital, where they were treated for malaria, typhoid, acute flu, skin diseases and other ailments.

Furthermore, these children were dirty and smelly—they operated in dumpsites, and some had not showered or changed clothes for many months—but I sat close to them and listened to their stories. Whenever they were happy, especially after I had delivered food to them, they would hold my hand, brush themselves against me, pull me around, climb on my shoulders, struggle for my attention, play with me, and do all manner of things that ended up getting me dirty like them. When I went back home one might imagine that I had been rolling in a pool of mud. My clothes were extremely soiled. Furthermore, these children were infected with crawling pests such as lice, and I ended up catching lice too.

These are some of the minor challenges that I faced while reaching out to the street children, but they never deterred me from focusing on my main goal of rescuing and rehabilitating them.

For example, each time I returned home from Sosiani River, my clothes had to be thoroughly disinfected. However, to control this situation among the children, I would bring them soap and advise them to bath by the river and wash their clothes. This ensured that we all remained clean. This was a tall order for some of them, who had a phobia of water, but others took it with enthusiasm and practised some personal hygiene.

After continued interaction with the street children—playing, greeting and holding hands—I began getting itchy hands, especially at the back of my palms. My irritated skin began peeling off. I constantly kept scratching my hands. I later found out that I had contracted scabies, an extremely itchy skin disorder that spreads from one person to another through close skin-to-skin contact.

Medical experts say scabies is contracted from prolonged hand-holding with an infected person. It is caused by a parasitic infestation on one's skin. Itching is the main symptom of scabies. It is often severe and tends to be in one place at first (often the hands) and then spreads to other parts of the body. If the skin becomes infected with bacteria, it becomes red, inflamed, hot and tender. Scabies can stay in your skin forever if not treated. It can be cured by applying a medicinal cream or lotion as prescribed by the doctor. My condition persisted for a while, and I went to the hospital for treatment, but I was not immediately healed. I lived with it for over 10 years.

In my talks with church members, business people and local leaders whom I interacted with regularly, I kept insisting that they consider doing something to end the plight of the street children. I considered street life an operations ground for the devil where vulnerable children were going to be wiped out one by one. I wanted my friends to join with me in helping the street children. To me, it was obvious.

But it was not so obvious to others.

To my surprise, my business and church friends were blinded. They did not have the vision to see street children for who they could become. Instead, they could only see the street children for who they were. It was as if a veil covered their eyes. They did not, or would not, hear the truth that was so easily within their grasp. They pushed the truth out of reach.

Sometimes fear can have such a grip on life. This is what happened to my friends. No doubt they felt threatened that their comfortable life might be in jeopardy should they choose to act on truth. They wanted to hang on to something that was not real. It reminds me of the words of our Lord: "Whoever wants to save their life will lose it, but whoever loses their life for me will find it" (Matthew 16:25).

I felt immense pressure as I chose to let go of my life. But when I did—when I released everything into God's hands and surrendered it all—it was then that I found the life for which I was created.

And even though most of my friends abandoned me, the Lord assured me that I was following His call to help in the restoration of street children living in such deplorable conditions.

As I continued to visit them, I realized that the street was full of different types of children. There were those who had been abandoned and had no idea where they came from and those that had opted to rummage in the streets and dumpsites for something to eat because their poor parents could provide nothing at all.

The faces in the streets showed a combination of despair and anger. Despair because their lives were empty. They hardly ate anything. They never went to school. They had no food. No clothes. No place to call home. They hoped for nothing.

They were angry at everything and everybody around them. Perhaps some of them thought that the smartly dressed people who ate good food and threw some away, those who bought many nice things in supermarkets, drove nice cars and lived in comfortable homes, had contributed to the negative plight of the street children. You could sense a feeling of *them-against-us*, the perception that *those people are prospering at our expense*.

Through God's support, favour and inspiration, I never gave up on my rescue mission, even when things seemed impossible. As I continued interacting with street children by giving them food and showing them love, I gradually started taking charge of their lives. Unlike other days when I had been staying around them as a silent observer, I now started telling them what to do and how to do it. I even took the lead in lighting the fire in the evening by using some of the old motor vehicle tires. They now saw me as one of them.

One evening, after everyone had eaten, I opened our conversation by asking them, "Who is God? Who knows God? Do you know God's commandments?" These questions made me realize that the children knew nothing about Christianity or only had a vague idea. Typically, religious concepts were taught at home, church and school. Unfortunately, the street children did not belong to a home, church or school. They had little knowledge about God. So I took it as my duty to help them know and understand God right there in the difficult circumstances in which they lived. I became their teacher and led them in singing songs and praising God.

We sang simple Christian songs together every evening before praying. I told them many stories about God and His love for humanity. One of the stories that I loved to tell them was how Jesus fed thousands of people with five loaves of bread. Stories helped them hear the truth of God, which inspired them to believe for great things. This is why I also told them stories of people who were once poor but rose into greatness by trusting in God. This gave them further encouragement to know that God could and would use them. I told them many stories of hope based on biblical teachings Most importantly, they were encouraged to come to know, love and worship God. I even invited them to our church on Sundays.

Whenever conflict arose among the children, I acted as an arbitrator. I would stop them from bullying, fighting and injuring each other, and I solved many cases of conflicts among them. Fighting and abusing each other was the order of the day. There were cases of organized fights between rival groups, often fighting for food or control of a particular street or dumpsite. Whenever I heard of such cases, I warned them about the dangers of fighting and preached to them about love. I told them to regard each other as brothers and sisters who were suffering the same fate and to help each other. I taught them about love, honesty, the importance of not keeping grudges and to refrain from stealing.

"God wants to save your life and make you great people. But if you commit crimes, if you fight and steal, if you continue being selfish, He will not rescue you," I told them. Some took my words seriously; others were inattentive and made fun of what I said. Sometimes I would give them a rather tall order. "If you get any food today, go and share it with other street children in town, Langas or Huruma, then come and tell me." I considered the art of sharing and exercising love as one way of reducing hostilities among street children.

In my teachings, I told the children that the difference between God and Satan was that God loves peace and Satan loves fighting. I told them that God loves sharing, while Satan is selfish. I told them that God is honest, while Satan is a thief. I reiterated to them that those who love God will promote a peaceful existence and those who love Satan will fight other people. Using the Bible verse John 14:23, I explained that "anyone who loves me will obey my teaching. My Father will love them, and we will come to them and make our home with them."

My intention was to enable them to know God, reduce the levels of crime in the streets, create some order and exercise love in their lives, in spite of the disorderly environment in which they lived. In the early hours of the morning I would go back home a very tired man, but I kept asking God to sustain my plans of making a difference in their lives.

Generally, the street children were difficult to work with. They had already formed a solid subculture, and it was not easy to convince them to leave it. They were strong in what they believed in. They had no hope in life, and they knew the world was full of bad people and that to get anything one had to step on others. Unfortunately, most, if not all, of the things they believed in were wrong. They had known a lot of wrong things in the streets. They had experienced many forms of abuse and were skilled at abusing others. They had matured in crime and could even kill, even as they also were in danger of being killed. Worst of all, they had given up hope. They did not care about anything. Not even themselves. They would throw foul words at anybody carelessly. They had nothing to lose in this world. A very dangerous attitude, indeed.

Having received a first-hand experience regarding the appalling lives of the street children, I concluded that everything that went on in the streets was against God's teachings and wishes for humankind. I looked at street life as an operation ground for the devil where evil spirits were nurtured and spread to cause havoc. As a member of God's army, I endeavoured to rescue as many children as possible from the streets and return them back to God. Every time I prayed to God I would hear Him tell me, "Charles, you have seen the suffering of the children. You now have to move fast and make a change. Bring them all back to Me." This message kept recurring for many days.

Bring them all back to Me.

I chose to rescue the street children because they struck me as the most vulnerable of all needy groups. Compared with other needy groups, the street children faced all manner of dangers, including diseases, prostitution, crime, drug abuse, HIV/AIDS, murder, starvation and attacks by wild animals. They simply stared at many dangers. In my assessment, this was a ruined group, and they were in desperate need of help.

God spoke to me about all of their troubles and called me to intervene in their lives. He had sent me to reach out to the poor and lost ones and return them to His fold. Every time I prayed to the Almighty God, He reminded me about this call.

In the long run, I never gave up, even when faced with numerous challenges. I persisted in my attempts to change the thinking of street children. They saw themselves as useless. They also viewed the world as a place of battles: stealing, fighting, killing, and being killed. They never knew love. I kept preaching to them about loving one another, being hopeful for a good future and leading a righteous life, despite the incredible challenges they faced. Most of them did not understand me. Some would stare at me blankly with a look suggesting *It is impossible*. Others showed outright rebellion, while the majority simply laughed off what I said.

With time they started taking my words seriously, and I became their leader in the streets. They gradually became attached to me. The public, who watched from a distance, did not understand my relationship with the street children. Many people who knew me as a respectable businessman and church elder started doubting my sanity. There were murmurs that "Mulli must be out of his mind. He sits with chokoras at dumpsites each night...Something must be wrong with him. Those children are robbers and prostitutes; what is he doing with them? What are they discussing? Someone should talk to him."

Many people could not believe that a rich man in his right mind could do what I was doing. They argued that no sensible man would leave the comfort of his house to spend time with dirty, smelly street children by the riverside in often cold and rainy conditions. Even fellow Christians in our church felt that something was wrong.

One Sunday morning, members of our church were stunned when I turned up for the service with about 40 street children. Some worshippers could not stand a huge group of dirty, smelly children coming into the church. They hated what I was doing. There was a brief commotion and an outright show of disapproval. Eventually, the dirty children were told to sit outside. Perhaps they were considered unfit for the church.

The church's response made me understand what some people, including my fellow Christians, think about the lowly in the society. I learned that human beings mostly prefer to associate with the clean and well-to-do in society. Nobody likes the poor. I had interacted with these children and shared with them about God, His love for humanity and His treatment of everyone as equal. They were ready to accept Him as their saviour through the church. I had told them that it does not matter to God who you are or how you are.

I knew that these children wore smelly clothes, but I was convinced it was our responsibility to clothe them decently and make them clean. These children had all sorts of dirt on them, but it was up to us to make a difference. By bringing them to church, I was expecting the members to embrace them and help clean them physically, emotionally and psychologically. I expected people to pledge clothes and food.

These street children had been subjects of condemnation everywhere. Whenever they stood outside a shop or supermarket, the security people chased them away for fear that they would steal from the shoppers. Whenever they showed up near a hotel, perhaps hoping to be given something to eat, they were told to keep off the grounds and stop disturbing people who were eating. They were never welcome anywhere they went. This turned them into outcasts. Now, imagine the impact that could have been made on these children if the church had received them with genuine love and hugs?

I believe that many people, even those in church, do not understand the essence of loving and worshipping God. They think that everything starts with praising God, worshipping Him, praying, tithing and leading pious lives. But as the Bible says in James 2:14–17, faith without actions is dead. God looks more at our actions toward others than our words. James states,

> What good is it, my brothers and sisters, if someone claims to have faith but has no deeds? Can such faith save them? Suppose a brother or a sister is without clothes and daily food. If one of you says to them, "Go in peace; keep warm and well fed," but does nothing about their physical needs, what good is it? In the same way, faith by itself, if it is not accompanied by action, is dead.

It is further said that the best way to judge a society is to look at how it handles people who can do or offer nothing in return. If you wish to know the true character of people, look at the way they handle those who cannot do anything for them in return. Many church elders would rush to wait at the door whenever politicians said they were coming to church, but most were unwilling to look twice at miserable and helpless groups such as the street children. These politicians, some of whom stole from the public and even orchestrated violence, were given high priority in most cases, unfortunately, because of the huge offering they would give. But because the unkempt and smelly children could not give any money, nobody wanted to associate with them or have them around.

The brethren forgot that the Church was meant to rehabilitate and restore lost souls back to God. They hardly understood that God strongly judges us according to whatever we do to others, rather than what we say or pretend to be. Our actions speak louder than our words or intentions about our how close or far we are from God. Jesus wanted His disciples to embrace this conviction, as captured in Matthew 25:40–45:

> "The King will reply, 'Truly I tell you, whatever you did for one of the least of these brothers and sisters of mine, you did for me.' Then he will say to those on his left, 'Depart from me, you who are cursed, into the eternal fire prepared for the devil and his angels. For I was hungry and you gave me nothing to eat, I was thirsty and you gave me nothing to drink, I was a stranger and you did not invite me in, I needed clothes and you did not clothe me, I was sick and in prison and you did not look after me.' They also will answer, 'Lord, when did we see you hungry or thirsty or a stranger or needing clothes or sick or in prison, and did not help you?' He will reply, 'Truly I tell you, whatever you did not do for one of the least of these, you did not do for me.'"

My decision to bring street children to church did not go down well with some of the leaders, and I was reprimanded for my "insensitive" actions. I was asked why I never sought permission. This became the subject of conversation for a long time.

While the church and members of the public considered me to be a crazy man because of my close relationship with street children, the police saw me as a gang leader who was using children (or intended to use them) for illegal purposes. They claimed they had observed me bringing food to and spending time with the street children at Sosiani River. The police suspected that I had used the children in criminal activities, though they could not provide evidence. They did not believe that I was giving food to these children out of goodwill; they believed it was some form of incentive or reward so that the children would commit something sinister on my behalf. According to the police, there was nothing good to be shared with these apparent wretched members of society.

One night when it was almost midnight I sat at the Sosiani River fire with the children. After I had given them food, they were laughing and telling me all manner of stories when suddenly the police came and arrested me. It had rained heavily, and I was seated close to the fire, listening to the children, when men in dark coats approached quickly and handcuffed me. Many street children were regular victims of police harassment, and when they saw security men arrive, they scattered in various directions.

I was taken to the Eldoret police station, where I was detained and then interrogated for over two hours to explain the reason behind my close association with street children, whom they termed "stubborn criminals." The police saw me as a conspirator in their criminal activities. "Are you luring them into crime? Are you using them for selfish interests? What do you discuss with them?" They asked endless questions.

The police made numerous allegations, saying that street children who were criminals mainly operated under some form of command from a malicious godfather (in this case, me). They concluded that in arresting me they had apprehended a commander of a criminal gang suspected to have been waylaying passersby at night, pickpocketing and breaking into shops, among other crimes.

I did not struggle to plead my innocence. I just told them that I was simply showing love to abandoned children and making them feel appreciated as human beings.

I listened to the police allegations and pitied them. I wished they knew that I was actually making great strides in dissuading the children from engaging in any form of crime or lawlessness. I explained to them that, just like Jesus came for the sinners, I had personally decided to go and sit with the street children, who were seen as very sinful, so that I could understand them, show them that someone cared and eventually get them out of lawlessness. I even preached to the police and told them that these poor children were not in the streets because of choice but because they lacked a father, a saviour, a helper and a guide. "If we give them an opportunity to enjoy life like other children, feel loved, and be part of a family, they will never go to the streets," I said.

Meanwhile, as the police looked at me with suspicion and interrogated me endlessly, the street children came to the station in large numbers and caused a commotion, demanding my release. They sat outside and sang some of the songs I had been teaching them. This, perhaps, reinforced the police belief that I was a gang leader. However, I was set free in the morning, and the children danced and celebrated within the police station. The officers watched in disbelief.

Despite the thoughts of many people being against my mission of rescuing the street children, I stood firm and continued with my plans because I knew God was fully with me. I could feel His presence in my work because within a short time the children who used to fight each other, talk badly about each other and steal had abandoned their criminal tendencies and were ready to hear about Jesus and God.

At this point, I learned that it was possible to rehabilitate street children and turn them into productive citizens and people of God. I had seen substantial signs that given an opportunity, street children would wish to lead normal lives where they could access food, shelter and education. What they needed was a brand new home, a brand new location and a brand new family.

And I was prepared to offer them that opportunity.

Chapter Four

THE BEGINNING OF MULLY CHILDREN'S FAMILY

Children can only progress when their basic needs of food, clothing, shelter, education, medical care and love are met. Without these, they do not have the tools to progress. They stay dependent on handouts, which actually serve to prevent them from advancing. A complete and holistic approach of a family setting in a home makes the biggest difference. This is the vision God has given me for MCF. It is a challenge, but it is the most effective way to win souls for Christ.

It was one thing for me to go out into the streets to meet with the children. That was already taking one step. Yet the call of God is always about further surrender and deeper love. And so I had to challenge myself by asking, what good did it do to only go out and simply see the street children and understand them?

> What good is it, my brothers and sisters, if someone claims to have faith but has no deeds? Can such faith save them? Suppose a brother or a sister is without clothes and daily food. If one of you says to them, "Go in peace; keep warm and well fed," but does nothing about their physical needs, what good is it? In the same way, faith by itself, if it is not accompanied by action, is dead. (James 2:14–18)

I started allowing boys to sleep in a small building on the large church property. This small building had served as the original church. When the congregation outgrew that little building, we started a much larger building. I was even appointed the overseer, not only over that new church but over 41 churches in the region.

This act of sheltering street boys in that little building marked a change in reaching out to street children. It guaranteed those few boys a safe place to sleep for the night. This brought with it so much confidence. Their minds were able to settle and be freed from the fear of what can happen at night. It seems like something so simple, yet for a street child, going through the day with the assurance of having a safe place for the night is revolutionary.

It enabled them to think beyond having to fight for their basic needs of food, clothing and shelter. They were in a position to change. To grow. To become who they were designed to be.

Still, it left me without a place to care for girls. I knew that I needed to expand the vision. To bring more children out of the slums and into the love of God. But how?

Again, the call of God is always deeper. More surrender results in more love. And so we began bringing children into our home. You can imagine the challenges that followed. Street children coming into a wealthy family's home. That was not an easy transition. The calling of God rarely is.

I brought more children into our home. It overflowed, and we were soon bursting at the seams. So I built dormitories in our backyard. I used sheet metal for the walls and roofs and built bunk beds out of wood. And these simple buildings, coupled with my sincere and deep love for the children, gave the boys and girls that desperately needed sense of security for their physical, mental and emotional well-being. Before children can truly change, they need to be in a safe environment where that change can be possible. That cannot happen in the street, where they are traumatized and live in constant fear of whether they will be beaten that evening, whether they will have food to eat, and whether there will be anyone with whom they can share their hearts.

But they did have that with me.

I did not simply want for them to have a roof over their head and food in their stomachs. I wanted them to feel the confidence and security that comes with being part of a family.

I continued to reach out to more and more destitute young people in the streets. The children I rescued came with all manner of horror stories. Their parents had died, some did not know where they came from or whether they even had parents, others had been beaten in the streets to near death, and some were victims of domestic violence, sexual abuse and many other unfortunate occurrences.

I saw the suffering and agony that the tiny children were going through in the streets, and I would feel anguish that comes with total sorrow.

As I rescued each child, my approach was to listen to their story, be patient with them, tell them a story about myself, show them love, and pray with them with a smile. Eventually, the children would feel love, open up, forget the past and pick up the pieces of their lives, regardless of their age or the sins they had committed. And the children would learn to forgive the sins committed against them.

I am glad that with God, nothing is too late, and no sins are too impossible for Him to forgive.

Personally, I consider the family the fabric of society where characters are nurtured and developed, where orderliness and brotherliness reign supreme, and where the love of God is greatly manifested. It is a unit where people care for one another, wish each other well and are ready and willing to stand by one another whatever the circumstances. These are some of the key privileges that most street children do not receive.

Thus when I started a children's home I chose to call it a *family* because all the children that I took in were going to be my children, and they would all call me Daddy. I was not going to be a shadowy sponsor but rather an ever-present loving father. My intention was to care and provide for them just like a father does for his children. My wife, Esther, became their mother, and she treated them as her children. My biological children became brothers and sisters to all the adopted ones. All the MCF children are cultured to see each other as brothers and sisters. The home has become such a big family. This is why we are called Mully Children's Family.

This was not a simple thing for my family members to accept. It definitely threw them off-balance. It abruptly interfered with the way of life they were used to. But I discussed the importance of accepting the will of God with my wife and children. I told them that it is God who put us in this world, and He has a purpose for each one of us. I explained to them that God's wish was to see many street children rescued and brought back to Him. And that He had chosen me to accomplish that mission for Him. Eventually, they all embraced the idea of MCF and agreed to join me in welcoming street children into our life and home.

Besides the passion I have had for many years for helping the needy in society, I was driven to rescue street children because I felt that the lives they led in the streets made them appear less human, whereas we are all equal in the eyes of the Lord.

The Bible in Genesis 4:1–9 teaches us to be our brother's keeper. This is an instruction from God that we should be mindful of other people's welfare, feel for them and help them with their problems. In Genesis, after Cain had killed his brother, Abel, the Lord appeared and asked Cain where Abel was. Cain's response was "I don't know...Am I my brother's keeper?" Yes, every man is his brother's keeper in that we are not to commit violent acts against others or allow others to commit violent acts if we can prevent it.

This sort of "keeping" is something God rightfully demands of everyone, on the grounds of justice and love. But Cain's reply indicated a total lack of love for another human being. It also showed the kind of selfishness that kills affection and gives rise to hatred. However, as Christians we are our brother's keeper. And the main way we do this is by exhibiting brotherly love towards others.

Galatians 6:2 says, "Carry each other's burdens, and in this way you will fulfill the law of Christ." Furthermore, Matthew 25:35 declares, "For I was hungry and you gave me something to eat, I was thirsty and you gave me something to drink, I was a stranger and you invited me in." It is in this light that I have always held a strong belief that if everyone took it as his or her responsibility to care about poor children, it would not be difficult to eradicate the street menace in Kenya.

Presently, we have a population of about 40 million Kenyans. Out of these, about 1 million are street children. That leaves us with about 39 million people able to have a place they call home. Out of these, at least 10 million are able to put food on the table and have a little left over to share with a neighbour. Mathematically, this means that if 1 in 10 people chose to support 1 child—by way of sponsoring them to be adopted into a nearby children's home—then the street menace could be eradicated. This is how we can handle the street children problem and be able to stand with one another as a nation, as human beings and as people who love God.

I started MCF by bringing in six children to live in my household. Most of them were girls. I chose them first because street life was too rough for them. The numbers of children gradually grew because word on the street spread: "Mulli rescues and helps the needy." Within a year I had brought close to 50 children to my compound. I constructed makeshift houses for them in my backyard. I even established a small school where they were taught basic morals and education, mainly focusing on lower primary grades.

The numbers continued to increase, and by 1995 I had over 300 children under my care. This created the need for expansion. I needed more space to build accommodation rooms for the children. I needed more land to grow food for them. I needed a big space for them to play. And so I chose to relocate them from Eldoret to Ndalani, Machakos. We later expanded and built another home in Yatta.

I had a luxurious home in Eldoret. But I left it and moved with the children to a place called Ndalani that was literally barren. We did not have a lot of infrastructural development there. The road network was poor. There was no electricity. And we did not yet have the opportunity to build suitable accommodations. Still I chose to relocate there. I trusted God for the provision of all the services that we needed. I felt more at peace in Ndalani than in Eldoret, where pessimistic friends kept bothering me with their "concerns" that I was undertaking something that I would regret later in life.

In my days as a businessman I would put on nice suits and drive a variety of cars, including a luxurious Mercedes Benz. But when I started the children's mission I operated mainly with a pickup truck and wore jeans, T-shirts and other casual clothes. This caused a raft of discussions among my friends in the church and in business circles, who talked about me as a man who had blown away his fortune "and now lives a miserable life." But personally, I felt more at home in my new casual lifestyle than in the old one, where I had everything nice but lacked peace of mind.

During this time of transition, I came to discover that humility and inner peace go hand in hand. The less compelled you are to try to prove yourself to others, the easier it is to feel peaceful inside. I felt that I was under no obligation to prove a point to anybody, and I lived my life the way God had directed me.

While in Eldoret, I was pleasantly surprised when I realized that the government of Kenya had been following the activities of MCF and it fully appreciated the work we were doing.

I came to learn this when I received information that Uasin-Gishu District Commissioner (DC) Ismael Chelang'a wanted to see me in his office. Those days, DCs were very powerful people in the district, and whenever you received their summons, you would ask yourself very many questions. Chelang'a was close to President Moi, and this made him even more powerful. His word was law in Uasin-Gishu. I kept asking myself several questions as I drove to his office. *Why does the DC want to see me? Is there anything wrong I have done?*

When I was ushered into his office, Chelang'a, a tall, black, well-built man, stood up and greeted me warmly and firmly. "Charles Mulli, I'm happy with what you are doing for the street children in this town. As a government, we appreciate your efforts and sacrifices, and we shall work with you improving the lives of our needy children," he said as his secretary served me tea. Our discussion that day centred on the importance of helping the needy children.

The DC later visited my home in Pioneer Estate and interacted with the children who were there. He arrived with National Director of Children Affairs Mr. Hussein. The two brought several gifts for the children, mainly foodstuff, blankets and clothing. The children were so happy to receive them. "Charles, in the case you have any problem, do not hesitate to come to my office, and we will discuss it," Chelang'a told me.

Out of this, Chelang'a and I became close friends, and I regularly visited him. We discussed a wide range of issues, mainly related to development and humanitarian assistance. He was a development-oriented man, and he never failed to outline some of his major plans in developing Eldoret town and the entire Uasin-Gishu district, which is now a county.

A few months later, I received information that the DC wanted to see me again. When I entered his office, Chelang'a went straight to the point. "Bwana Mulli, I have called you here to tell you that the government has set aside five acres of land to construct a children's home. However, because you have already established one, I want to give you that land so that you can construct a rescue home and manage it in conjunction with the government," he said. He paused for a while, perhaps to allow his words to sink in.

I liked what I was hearing, and I told him in clear words: "That is exactly what I have been expecting to hear from you all these years. The best way of solving an African problem such as the street children problem is to apply an African solution such as the one you are offering. Let us use the little local resources we have at our disposal in order to make a difference. We should not wait for assistance from abroad in order to help a suffering child next door. I'm ready to work with you to save the vulnerable children of this country from the agony that they go through."

I asked him about the ownership of the home, and Chelang'a suggested that it would be owned and run by MCF on behalf of the government. He even told me that the land title deed would be written in the name of MCF.

Chelang'a further said, "However, to me what matters most is not ownership of the home but the results that will come out from the home. I want you to manage the centre and help save the lives of the children of Kenya, most of whom are engaged in crime, prostitution and other forms of lawlessness."

I was really impressed with his sentiments. Essentially, he was trying to create a sort of public-private partnership. He told me that the land was located on the western side of the Huruma Estate near Kidiwa. We even toured the place with him and held a lengthy chat on how we could team up to support the needy children. I was so glad that the government and I were reading from the same script. With this land there was going to be substantial room for expansion, and I was sure more street children were going to benefit from the initiatives of MCF in conjunction with the government.

However, before these plans could be implemented, two factors developed that caused a substantial challenge. First, unfortunately, Chelang'a was moved from Eldoret in 1993 and made provincial commissioner of the Rift Valley Province. At this point, he could not intervene much regarding small matters of the Uasin-Gishu district.

Second, one of the missionaries who had stayed in Eldoret for close to a decade and had established a children's home there caused trouble for us. I had known him for a while, and in our interactions I discovered that he was using the issue of street children for self-glory. He liked painting a picture of himself as a saviour of street children in Kenya. Quite often he liked talking big in order to attract more funding from his home country. He had initially sought to take over MCF, but I refused because I realized he only wanted it for personal gain. This man could not believe that an African would dedicate his resources to helping poor Africans. Thus he kept prying into MCF's affairs to establish where we were getting money and all our support.

His actions against us continued. While in Eldoret, I had worked closely with Chelang'a to establish the Uasin-Gishu children's council, which I chaired. The missionary, however, was not happy about what we were doing. He disrupted our plans by using some people within the government to question our sincerity.

Then he went to the authorities behind my back, telling them that he was the main sponsor of MCF and not me and telling many people that Charles Mulli was an employee of MCF and that he was the owner. Being a talkative man who used to knock on every door and sing his own praises, he went ahead and told government officials to deal with him on matters regarding street children and not me. He convinced the government that if given the land, he would do greater things than me.

Surprisingly, perhaps because he was a *mzungu* (white person), most people in the government offices believed him, and essentially the plans to give the Eldoret facility to MCF went silent. I also came to learn that there were two centres of power when it came to managing public resources—the provincial administration and the municipal council. Chelang'a, who had been on my side, was part of the provincial administration. The mzungu sabotaged our idea by poisoning the municipal council officials, this after all the land was within the jurisdiction of the Eldoret municipality.

But somehow I had prepared myself to handle such people by not paying attention to them at all. So, when he interfered with the Kidiwa land issue, I chose not to fight back. I knew that he had the potential to derail us from our main goal, so I avoided him completely.

When I realized that this mzungu was quietly dragging MCF into a sideshow and creating cold wars, I quietly sought a way to expand our area in a quieter environment so we could concentrate fully on helping the needy children.

For the six years that I had lived with the children in Eldoret, I experienced numerous cases of children escaping from my home. It only took 15 minutes for them to travel back to the streets of Eldoret, where they would return to glue sniffing, drug abuse, petty theft and other undesirable engagements. On several occasions, I spent considerable time in Eldoret looking for children who had escaped and bringing them back to the rehabilitation centre. Thus one purpose of relocating to the countryside was to create a new and friendly environment—one that was far away from what they had grown acclimatized to in their towns and cities. I wanted them to forget about town life and concentrate on learning.

By faith—being sure of what we hope for and certain of what we do not see—I relocated from Eldoret to Ndalani with my huge family of over 300 children. Many years earlier I bought this 50-acre property with the intention of building a rural home for my retirement. But my plans changed. The Lord had other ideas. And it became the ideal place to plant MCF.

Finally, I acquired land in Ndalani and relocated there with all the children under my care. I wanted to keep away from supremacy battles and concentrate on helping these children the way God had instructed me to do. I also wanted a place where I could expand, build a school, start a hospital and engage in large-scale agriculture and many other things. Furthermore, I wanted to give MCF children an environment where they would be able to forget about street life and focus on learning.

At first, I desired to build a centre somewhere on the Athi River. I located very good land in Lukenya, not far from Daystar University. But that place did not have a sufficient water supply to enable us to practice massive agriculture through irrigation. I had intentions of growing enough food to feed all the children, who already numbered in the hundreds and continued growing each month. I did not have a lot of external funding to support MCF, but as a successful businessman I knew that sustainability projects would be more responsible than sitting back and waiting for well-wishers. So while I wanted to set up MCF in Lukenya because of its good road infrastructure, the lack of water held me back. And so I contemplated the Ndalani farm in Machakos that was close to a river.

Many people did not support my establishment of a children's home. At the start, I funded it 100 percent myself, and people thought I was biting off more than I could chew. Others argued that I should have sought external funding before I fully committed my time and resources into the charity. Some of my friends advised me to be careful not to spend a lot "because if things go wrong, you will need a fall-

back position." Personally, I fully trusted in God. I knew I was undertaking all this on His behalf, and I never doubted His ability to guide
MCF for generations to come.

So when I said I planned to relocate from Eldoret to Machakos, my
friends concluded that I was crazy. "How do you move from a town
where you own property and go where there is nothing? If anything,
many people are longing to move here and not the other way round," a
friend said. He took time to explain to me that Eldoret was a fast-grow-
ing cosmopolitan town full of opportunities. Plus, it had nice weather—
full of rain throughout the year—as opposed to semi-arid Machakos,
where it hardly rained. He talked about Eldoret as a major economic hub
linking Western Kenya, North Rift, Uganda and even Sudan. "We even
have an international airport! How do you, as a businessman, move
away from such a promising town?"

The pessimistic sentiments of such people made me question
myself: *Am I really doing the right thing?* I took time, prayed and told
God to stand by me because I was doing His work. "Let your will be
done, God," I prayed. In my heart I continued to be convinced that
these children would get proper rehabilitation and be able to focus on
their studies if I relocated them to the countryside, where rehabilitation
could take place uninterrupted. We moved ahead with our plans to relocate to Ndalani.

However, Ndalani was very hot, dry, bare and windy. By the time we
got there, it had not rained for the past seven years! Due to their total
reliance on rain-fed agriculture, the people could not successfully grow
any produce. They only waited for relief food from the government.
Living standards were deplorable, and their circumstances formed the
basis of the popular view that famine was killing people in Ukambani.

In Eldoret, we used to receive many visitors, especially members of
the Asian community, who visited us regularly to donate food and other
gifts to the children. But Ndalani was quite inaccessible, lying eight kilometres away from the nearest paved road that linked Thika and Garissa.
Nobody came to visit us. To some people, this was a life of total isola-
tion. To compound our misery, the children kept getting sick because of
unsafe drinking water and the unfriendly climate that was full of malaria-
carrying mosquitoes.

However, I chose not to complain about the misfortunes we were facing. I purposed to convince everybody to accept the situation facing us
and encouraged them to do whatever they could to make a difference.

I talked to my biological children, MCF children and my staff, urging them to join me in a massive tree-planting exercise in order to make a difference in the area. Planting and watering trees every morning and evening became our major preoccupation. We drew water from the river that ran through the MCF farm. Our main project was to engage in massive land reclamation and water conservation in order to create a favourable environment for sustainable farming. At the same time, I also ensured that we had safe drinking water by sinking a borehole, which we christened "Jacob's well."

Five years later, we had planted over 500,000 trees, and MCF Ndalani had changed into a cool, green place. By 2015, we had planted over two million trees, and Ndalani is now arguably one of the greenest places in Kenya. A friend once told me that if your eyes are closed and you are dropped in MCF Ndalani today, you will not imagine that you are in Ukambani. One would assume the location is in Central Kenya or the Rift Valley.

In our new home in Ndalani, I established some of the key projects that were paramount to the success of the children rescue mission. We started projects in the areas of education, counselling, mentorship, spiritual nourishment, outreach to communities, agriculture, sustainability and environmental management.

Under education, we established nursery, primary and secondary schools, as well as a vocational training centre. These were meant to enable our children to access education just like any other group in Kenya. Most of the children we rescued were immediately entered into some form of academic training. Because of our large numbers, coupled with the need to give our students close supervision, we chose to build a school instead of sending them to neighbouring schools. Some of our students were slow learners, and we feared they would not cope well outside of our care. Others were already in their teens, and we did not wish them to feel intimidated in attending class with children half their age.

Further, we established schools at MCF because we wanted to focus on other needs the children had in addition to education. Most of them did not know God; thus we dedicated a lot of class time to teaching the Word of God. We also dedicated substantial time to counselling sessions. Our aim was to ensure that these children came out strong morally, spiritually and academically.

We started by establishing the MCF Ndalani primary school, then the MCF Ndalani secondary school. We later opened MCF Yatta secondary school and a vocational training college. We also set up a primary and secondary school in Vipingo. By 2015, plans were in the final stages to establish MCF schools in Kitale and Lodwar.

Our schools have been doing exceptionally well in national examinations. Many MCF children have graduated and moved on to university to pursue degrees in medicine, engineering, education, media studies and other majors.

We began offering various vocational courses as a viable alternative to beneficiaries who opted not to pursue academic careers. These programs include vocational courses in tailoring, cooking, knitting, hairdressing, building and construction, among other forms of vocational training. The aim has been to empower everyone to do something for themselves and contribute positively to society. Most of the graduates of these courses are operating successfully as self-employed entrepreneurs in various parts of Kenya. Though they were once destitute, a good percentage of them have families and are happily involved in contributing to the Kenyan economy.

In order to create a sense of responsibility in our children, we started counselling and mentoring sessions at MCF. We have counsellors and caregivers at MCF who spend a considerable amount of time mentoring the children. These are supported by our pastors and teachers, who are always ready to help the children adjust and cope with life in their new home.

Our model is to teach love by showing love to the children. We teach them to pray by praying with them. We teach them courtesy by exercising it ourselves. We teach them to have faith by living a life of faith ourselves. We teach them more by example than by simply telling them "You must do this...You can't do that."

As part of our holistic rehabilitation process, we provide spiritual nourishment to all our beneficiaries, from children in kindergarten to adults in vocational training. This program is steered by a team of dedicated resident pastors. It involves daily devotion sessions. The children read and internalize biblical messages. It also involves preaching and prayer groups, interactive Bible studies, and participation in choir and music, as well as other activities. As a result we have been able to put together one of the best evangelical choirs in the region.

At MCF we practice modern agriculture as the backbone of our sustainability projects. Even though Ndalani and Yatta are located in a semi-arid region, we have invested in irrigation and green house farming.

Through this, we produce food for our children and also sell the surplus to generate income for the daily management and needs of the centre. We are one of the few individual exporters of French beans in Kenya, having satisfied the stringent standards required by the European market. Since 2001, MCF has been exporting French beans, tomatoes and other produce to European markets on a weekly basis.

We also use our farm to train local farmers in proper farming methods, free of charge. In an effort to improve farming in arid and semi-arid areas and create sustainability, we established an annual exhibition at MCF Yatta aimed at educating farmers on good farming practices that guarantee better yields.

The inaugural event was held on July 4, 2014. The theme of the show was "Sustainable Food Security in Arid and Semi-Arid Lands." Farmers were taught about soil and water conservation, land preparation and farm management, crop diseases and pest management and control, crop health and management, crop harvesting and post-harvest management. We opened our doors and gave local residents a free invitation to visit us any time for learning sessions.

As a humanitarian organization, we consider sharing knowledge as one aspect of reaching out and empowering the community. Thus, this event was a knowledge-sharing forum that enabled farmers and other key players in the agricultural sector to learn some of the modern farming techniques that could guarantee food security, especially in arid and semi-arid areas. The aim of the exhibition was to show the farmers that despite the harsh climatic conditions, people can produce enough food to sustain their families and even have a surplus for sale.

We told the attendees that this was possible through massive tree planting. This would stop their total reliance on rain-fed agriculture and help them embrace irrigation and green house farming techniques.

"MCF is a practical example that we can manage our environment in spite of the harsh climatic conditions. We are located in a place with little rainfall throughout the year, but through a concerted environmental management program, MCF has been turned into a cool green environment full of trees. This has been achieved through great investment in tree planting," I told the farmers.

As part of our key plans to increase the number of trees in Machakos county and change our environment, MCF decided to approach schools, because we believe that young people have the energy and enthusiasm to take an idea, run with it and steer it to produce the desired results. They do not have a prejudiced mindset, and to them everything is possible. Many people may had given up on planting trees in Ukambani because it's too dry and everyone believed trees could not grow here, but the children are ready to take the initiative and usher in a green environment in Machakos without depending on the rain.

To spur them on, we started the Dr. Charles Mulli Environmental Award, mainly in Yatta sub-county, which recognizes students who have excelled in tree planting. This award promotes responsibility and leadership initiatives among the youth. The goal of the award is to promote community action through schools in environmental conservation. It has a wide range of objectives that include encouraging tree planting in schools and homes, encouraging water harvesting and conservation activities, and creating a sustained awareness of environmental conservation matters.

For many years now I have had a great passion for changing and improving our environment. After planting close to three million trees in Ndalani and Yatta, we have transformed our land from dry and barren to green and productive. Through this, I have come to believe that human beings can systematically work on their environment and transform it to the desired standards in spite of the degree of aridness that exists in a place. Because of our persistent afforestation, MCF has been turned into a place conducive to farming and human habitation.

As a result of our concerted efforts in tree planting, the United Nations Environmental Program (UNEP) conferred on me the Billion Tree Campaign Award, which recognizes people who make efforts in greening the environment.

In light of this we started holding annual events for school children, focusing on proper environmental management and behaviour change. We held such an event in October 2014, where the participants planted over 3,000 seedlings at MCF Yatta. The event brought together about 1,000 students from schools in Machakos county and the neighbouring areas. The youth were later urged to go back to their homes and schools and ensure they plant more trees in order to create a positive climatic change in the semi-arid Ukambani region. A similar event took place in October 2015 at MCF Yatta.

Our coming together enabled us to share with these young people the good practices that would guarantee them a good future. We decided to hold their hands and walk together with them into a better future. As the Bible says in Proverbs 22:6, "Start children on the way they should go, and even when they are old they will not turn from it."

This initiative has sparked a flurry of environment-related activities in the region and beyond. Students in Machakos have planted many trees, both at school and at home, and they are taking good care of them. Besides our role of saving lives, we have strongly embraced the role of saving our environment. The MCF tree seedlings propagation and production unit has been able to distribute tens of thousands of seedlings to the schools and community for planting. We intend to keep increasing this supply.

In order to ensure that the trees survive hardships, we demonstrated to the youth how to plant a seedling three feet deep, add some manure, and then water it. With constant watering, preferably twice a week or even more frequently, the trees grow to a height of about two metres within a year. In about three years, the once bare land will be fully covered with green. This is how we managed to create a forest at MCF.

Along this great journey, MCF has been blessed with incredible friends from around the world. I marvel at how God has raised up people from all walks of life who show their compassion for the ministry. I cherish the many, many friends who have sacrificially given of their time, talents and money for our ministry. I am always so touched by how people from countries so far away give to MFC with such generosity. Many of those who give do not know the children at MCF, yet their hearts have been touched and they give anyway. Many have taken time off of work to volunteer and help at MCF. Others have taken great effort to share the vision of MCF in their home country. This generosity amazes me because many people who give do not have a historical connection to me. They have no previous direct connection with Africa. At some point they heard about MCF for the first time and they give of themselves as if they have known us their entire lives. Truly MCF extends far beyond the borders of our home in Kenya. Mully Children's Family extends to the hearts of our friends around the world who have helped to make MCF possible. Where would MCF be without them? I could not imagine. It reminds me that MCF is not simply a place in Africa. It is truly a mindset of compassionate, God-given love that binds us together around the world in reaching people with the mission God has placed on my heart.

From our beginning by caring for street children in that little house on the church property to bringing them into our home in Eldoret and later branching out to MCF Ndalani, MFC Yatta and beyond, we have seen a common thread through everything. What has enabled MCF to grow is that Christ has done all the work through us step by step. And the way in which Christ operates through us—through anyone—is by faith. And it is this key aspect—the faith we have in Christ—that has made this all possible.

Chapter Five

MY JOURNEY OF FAITH

There are many different ways in which we can perceive and handle various undertakings and challenges in life. Some look at life as a predetermined race where winning or losing has already been cast in stone. Nothing can be added; nothing can be removed. They believe that we live in a fateful world where our destiny is already sealed by powerful external forces, meaning that whatever one struggles to do in life adds up to nothing. Individuals with such a mentality often take the "wait and see" approach regarding many things they do and the challenges they face in life. Perhaps this explains why we often see many people stick their heads in the sand like the proverbial ostrich, hoping that something good will happen after all. Such people believe that they are mere observers in life (they consider themselves not capable of making any change) and are always hoping that somebody somewhere will someday emerge and make a difference. Such people often like using the phrase "it is not possible."

Further, there are two groups of people: ever-cautious operators and risk-takers. Ever-cautious ones always prefer to play it safe in everything they undertake. They do not question or contribute much. They prefer to maintain the status quo and keep things the way they are. Such highly cautious people mainly operate with the known and hardly venture into the unknown. On the other hand, risk-takers have the courage to question what is not going right and have the motivation to go ahead and do whatever they can in order to make a difference, however insignificant. Risk-takers choose to pursue a particular path regardless of the uncertainties or dangers that lie ahead. Such people do not fear the unknown.

 I prefer to look at life as a hill that we ought to climb and literally overcome. I believe that our destinies are in our hands and we have to work hard to achieve the desires of our hearts. Nothing is impossible, provided we stand up and face it head on.

When I started the Mully Children's Family I didn't have a clear picture of what it would eventually become. As the numbers kept growing and more children kept lining up to join the centre, I didn't know where I would get the resources to meet all of their needs. However, I never allowed the fear of the unknown to grip me. I did not allow myself to think "it is not possible." I did not collapse under the weight of fears and worries. But by the grace of God, I took the risk and chose to forge ahead regardless of the numerous uncertainties that surrounded this risky venture. I was just delighted that God was on my side, and I took the journey of faith without asking questions, doubting or thinking "what if."

Hebrews 11 teaches us about trusting God. In this chapter, the meaning of faith is explained through the actions of people like Abraham, Noah and Moses. It reads,

> Now faith is being sure of what we hope for and certain of what we do not see. This is what the ancients were commended for. By faith we understand that the universe was formed at God's command, so that what is seen was not made out of what was visible. By faith Abel offered God a better sacrifice than Cain did.

As a man who believes in and has witnessed God's great powers, I know that He conquers all manner of challenges. I knew God would create a way where there seemed to be no way, just like He separated the waters of the Red Sea and allowed His people to cross over from Egypt on the way to Canaan. I never doubted God's power, because I knew He is capable of performing great miracles. When I established MCF I did so because I serve God, not man. Thus I was sure God would not allow His ordained mission on earth to fail. I depended on Him to show the way and provide resources.

As I began God's mission of rescuing street children and helping the needy, I was guided by Isaiah 43:1–3:

> But now, this is what the LORD says—he who created you, Jacob, he who formed you, Israel: "Do not fear, for I have redeemed you; I have summoned you by name; you are mine. When you pass through the waters, I will be with you; and when you pass through the rivers, they will not sweep

over you. When you walk through the fire, you will not be burned; the flames will not set you ablaze. For I am the LORD your God, the Holy One of Israel, your Savior."

With such reassurance from the Almighty God, I continued running MCF without fear or doubt, because I knew I was undertaking God's will. I believed God had called me by name to undertake a special duty to care for humankind on His behalf, and He would not allow us to drown in the river or get burned by the fire. I believed He would protect us from all forms of calamities, and that is exactly what He has been accomplishing for us.

There is a saying "Don't tell God how big your storm is; tell the storm how big your God is." On many occasions we were faced with numerous difficulties: lack of resources, sickness among the children, sabotage from external forces, obstacles from corrupt government officials (especially when I went to register MCF schools) and many other challenges. But I did not care how difficult or impossible the journey seemed. All I knew was that the Lord was going to see me through all the hills and valleys as I trudged along.

I knew that the more difficult things get, the stronger God becomes. He was carrying me in His arms, and I knew He would safely take me forward so that I could accomplish His desires for humankind on earth. With faith in your heart, you will move mountains. When fear fills your heart, mountains will move you. I chose to be a mountain mover.

Through His love and guidance—and our belief in Him—we have not lacked food at MCF; we have been able to save many souls and restore them back to Him. We have been able to heal hurting souls. We have restored shattered dreams. We have given hope to the hopeless. We have paid millions of shillings for university tuition fees for our children. We have been able to change the environment in which we live in. And most importantly, we have been able to spread God's love far and wide among the people we interact with.

As the Lord says in Jeremiah 7:23, "Obey me, and I will be your God and you will be my people. Walk in obedience to all I command you." Here the Lord calls on us to trust Him and trust His ultimate power. He calls upon us to obey Him by keeping His words and commandments. He promises to never forsake us. We should cast our burdens upon Him and allow Him to work for us, through us. Even when things get tough and all the roads seem to lead nowhere, we should not waiver in our trust in the Lord. This has been my guiding principle in life.

As I grew in faith, I realized that God has used my early experiences to shape my character. Looking back at my early days in life, I see that I started trusting God to undertake the impossible at a very young age. At home we lived one day at a time, never sure from where the next meal would come. But I was sure that somehow we would get something to eat. We were not sure of tomorrow, but I trusted God that tomorrow would turn out well. I would borrow food from neighbours, and this made me look bothersome to some people. It created in me an inferiority complex, and this caused me to feel intimidated. I survived through God's mercy, all the while hoping for a better tomorrow.

Even though I did not have a meaningful formal education to guarantee me lucrative employment, I still believed I was headed for greatness. I felt a strong hope about the future. My family owned nothing, but I was sure that God was soon going to lift me from rags to riches. I could not explain how, but I was sure that He could. I kept trusting and believing in Him. I cast my worries onto Him who cares. This became the benchmark of my success story.

Within a couple of years, my trust in God started yielding fruit. At a time when it looked like there was going to be nothing meaningful for me in this world, God continually provided a means of employment. And at each job God equipped me with experience and skills that I would later need in establishing MCF.

As the years passed, I continued getting better employment opportunities and better income. And to crown it all, everything that I touched—especially the businesses that I engaged in—produced tremendous positive results. My businesses flourished more than I had expected. All this was because of my deep faith and trust in God. I started trusting him as a teenager, and for over 50 years I have never doubted God's abilities, and He has never let me down. The challenges in life and the realization that God was on my side gave me the ability to move on.

Chapter Six

THE PLIGHT AND REDEMPTION
OF THE STREET CHILDREN

Many developed nations have put in place strong mechanisms—supported by the government and private citizens—to ensure that the less privileged in society are helped to lead normal lives and are not forced to live in the streets. Philanthropy toward the poor is prevalent. However, despite many efforts, according to United Nations statistics (2013), there are over 100 million street children in the world, with the majority living in Africa and parts of Asia.

There are a number of factors that cause a child to live in the streets, mainly social and economic. Most of the children in the streets have been chased away from their home by violence, drug and alcohol abuse, the death of a parent, family breakdown, lack of support from their extended family, war, natural disaster or simply socioeconomic collapse.

Difficult economic conditions coupled with the breakdown of the past social fabric has caused destitute children to resort to the street as their only source of refuge. In Africa, it used to be customary for destitute children to be hosted and taken in by members of the extended family or even total strangers. In the current situation, however, these scenarios hardly exist. Most of the street children become idle in the streets, hoping someone will give them something to eat. Others are forced to eke out a living on the streets, scavenging, begging and hawking in the slums in order to survive.

Each child comes from a disadvantaged situation. Street life is terrible and dehumanizing. Children walk around with glue bottles essentially stuck to their noses while at the same time abusing drugs. It strips the children of their dignity and human values. It exposes them to numerous dangers and literally detaches them from the rest of the society. Such children lead miserable lives. They do not have access to food, shelter, education, parental love and guidance, religious awareness, a clean and healthy environment or many other fundamental human requirements.

I have also come to realize that there are various categories of street children. For example, there are those who take refuge on the streets during the day but return to some form of family at night. Then there are those who permanently live on the street without a family network. The former category are children with parents—or in most cases a single parent—who cannot afford to feed them or who are alcoholics and have abandoned their parental responsibilities. In many slums across Kenya and all over Africa, many parents do not know how their children eat or where they sleep. Children are told to "go out" and look for means of survival by whatever means are possible. Sometimes this involves stealing. It is a never-ending struggle for them to make ends meet.

The second category of permanent street dwellers is those who are totally alone. They know no family. Some of them do not know how they got to the streets. They just found themselves there, having been abandoned while still very young. These children are vulnerable to numerous forms of abuse and exploitation. They live in the streets, hide under bridges, wander through dumpsites and reside in dingy places. Most of them end up dying in the streets through mob justice, fighting among themselves, drug abuse, gang rivalry and diseases. Many street children have been killed by members of the public for engaging in petty theft.

These are realities that MCF has encountered over the past 25 years. We have rescued children from the streets, and their stories have been very moving and shocking. The tales of what they went through can best be described as horrific.

Over the years I have noticed that the types of problems the street children face have remained the same. However, there is a sharp difference in the magnitude of the problems. Drug trafficking is more advanced than when we first began. Children are consuming harder drugs. Prostitution is more open. And the vast scale of these problems is increasing in both urban and rural settings.

But as the saying goes, "all is well that ends well." Despite a difficult past, most of the children we rescued from the streets have gone on to become great achievers in life. I'm happy that our children have never disappointed us in terms of academic and social discipline. They have been able to remain focused on their studies until completion, while at the same time exercising the virtues that we teach and model at MCF, mainly respect, hard work, obedience, diligence and trust in God.

Despite great suffering, there are many stories of hope. For instance, we rescued George from the streets of Eldoret. We took him to primary school, and he later proceeded to high school (still with MCF schools) and passed his exams well. He joined the University of Nairobi for a bachelor's degree in medicine and surgery. He graduated in 2013 with first class honours. He later earned a post at a government hospital in Murang'a. His story is a typical case of rising from grass to grace. He was born in Timboroa, Uasin-Gishu county, to a single mother with four children. His mother did not hold a professional job. She had dropped out of school in lower primary. She worked as a casual farm labourer to feed her children. They were mere survivors who lived from hand to mouth.

Their home village was hit hard by tribal clashes, especially during the 1992 elections. Things took a turn for the worse when one afternoon they heard screams all over the village. They peered through the window and saw a group of men armed with arrows attacking homes in the neighbourhood. It was a chilling experience, especially for young children like George. Many houses were set ablaze that day.

George's uncles and other neighbours armed themselves and went out to face the attackers. One came back bleeding heavily with an arrow stuck in his left arm. The rest were all killed. The family could not stay in Timboroa any longer. They relocated to the Burnt Forest market, where they thought they would be safe. Even there they received threats of an impending attack. George's mother then courageously gathered her children in the evening and walked all the way to Eldoret, about 40 kilometres away. They arrived the following morning, tired, hungry, angry, dejected and hopeless. But perhaps they were happy that the horror of political and tribal violence had been left behind them. They felt safe in the city.

They lived in a slum in Eldoret. However, they could not afford the rent—about KSh100 per month. So they kept shifting houses regularly to evade the landlords, who would come to collect the money at the end of the month. They would live in a house and move out just as the end of the month approached. Meanwhile, George and his elder brothers would go out in the street to collect papers and metals from dumpsites. Then they would sell them at very low prices to garages and other businesspeople.

As fate would have it, their mother later passed on after a short illness. By then George was eight years old and full of anger at the world. He and his siblings became street children with no food, no education, no hope and no future.

A year later I met them in the streets. I listened to their moving story, and I took them to MCF, which I had just started. Here they found love, care and friendship, as well as spiritual and even psychological nourishment. I kept telling them about the importance of respecting God and taking their studies seriously. I later moved them to Ndalani, Machakos.

In 2002, George completed his Kenya Certificate of Primary Education (KCPE) at the MCF primary school in Ndalani, where he scored impressive marks. He joined MCF secondary and scored an A- in KCSE. I then secured his admission to the University of Nairobi to pursue a bachelor's degree in medicine and surgery. In 2013, George graduated with first class honours. His position at the government hospital in Murang'a is a testimony to his achievements.

George's eldest sister completed KCSE in MCF and immediately received a scholarship to the UK, where she studied accounting. Kariuki, the second born, went to a local university and studied accounting. He graduated in 2010 with first class honours. Kariuki was offered a job as a banker and is pursuing postgraduate studies. Ng'ang'a, the other brother, graduated from Maseno University in 2011 with a degree in marketing and presently works with a theatre arts firm in Nairobi.

This story illustrates how God can work miracles and lead people into greatness even when fellow human beings have written them off. People had written me off, too. I know what it is like to be at the bottom. I know what it is like to have life look hopeless. When you have nothing and when you have no one to believe in you, you can't even imagine that life can be different. You presume it is going to be nothing but a pointless, endless misery. But even when our own heart fails, God never fails. Even when it seems there is no hope from our perspective, there is always hope from God's perspective. Even when we can't understand His ways, He is working out His purpose. He enables us to have faith in Him despite any outside factors.

The case of Wilson is an example of how God is not limited by the circumstances where we are born. Wilson was born in the remote village of Lokori, Turkana. He was destined to grow up as a nomadic tribal warrior who would fiercely defend his family and community and protect his herd against any acts of banditry. Their home village was on the border of Turkana and West Pokot county, where cattle rustling was rampant.

Wilson was barely two years old when his father and other siblings were killed during a cattle rustling incident by suspected Pokot raiders. His departed relatives added to an ever-growing statistic of people who died (and continue to die) in the endless Pokot-Turkana clashes.

Following the death of his father, the young Wilson was relocated to the Lokori market with his mother and elder sister. There, life was very difficult. Food was extremely hard to come by. On many occasions they slept hungry. Their fate was further compounded by the unending famine and drought in Turkana.

Pushed by the difficult life at home, the young Wilson moved to Kainuk town, where he lived in the streets and begged for food from local residents and travellers who passed by. Kainuk is a transit town that links Kitale and Lodwar. It is a popular stopover for long-distance truck drivers, who are mainly heading to or coming back from southern Sudan. One day, as a truck stopped over in Kainuk en route to Kitale, Wilson climbed into the back and hid himself among a pile of sacks. Six hours later, the truck arrived in Kitale, where the little boy disembarked and continued with life in the streets. It was here that MCF rescued him and took him to our Ndalani home, in 1998. At MCF, he witnessed the love of a father and mother who cared about his well-being. At that time there were about 300 children living at MCF Ndalani. They came from different places and different tribes in Kenya, living together in harmony. He blended in well with his newfound brothers and sisters.

When he listened to some of their stories—where they had come from and what they had gone through—he immediately felt the connection orphans feel when they relate about the challenges they faced. They shared a similar past: desperation, destitution, rejection. But MCF brought them the true promise of a brighter future—a hope they so desperately needed. He felt at home. Now he had a complete family, a father and mother and many, many brothers and sisters.

Wilson was an ardent student. He completed secondary education at MCF and passed his KCSE exams with excellence. He was a very good mathematician. God opened a door for him to undertake further studies in Australia, where he acquired a bachelor's degree in computer science and later acquired a postgraduate diploma in business administration.

In 2006, he married an Australian named Claire, and they have been blessed with two children, Toby and Asha. They live in Ballarat, Australia, where Wilson works for one of the world's leading technology companies.

His story is a living testimony that even though people cannot choose the family they are born into, they can, regardless of their circumstances, achieve greater things far beyond their wildest imagination. The key to success is to remain steadfast in the Lord. There is peace in Him even when there is a wild storm around us. He will create a way where there seems to be no way. Furthermore, God promises that He will renew our strength and we can soar on wings like the eagles.

In Isaiah 45:2, God's promise is that He will go before us and level the mountains. He did that for Wilson and thousands of other MCF beneficiaries, and He can do it for anyone who believes in Him.

God's transforming love in the life of a child is a powerful indication to me of His active presence in our world. I am continually reminded that my God is not far off. He is near. He walks among us. And He desires to turn the hearts of each of His creation back to Him. I have seen incredibly hardened children respond to the love of Christ and shine as bright lights for Him. Nothing is impossible with God. And each time I see a child respond to the love of God I am so humbled that I can be part of God's restoring work here on earth.

Another MCF beneficiary who beat all the odds to achieve greatness is Mercy. Just like George, she graduated from the University of Nairobi with a bachelor's degree in medicine and surgery in 2013. She also was posted to a government hospital, in Kitui. Her story is one of resilience and hard work. She embodies the belief that you possess what you confess.

In 1996, she was only eight years old when her mother died while giving birth in their home village of Inyaanzani in Machakos county, in the neighbourhood of the MCF Ndalani centre. Her mother was single. Mercy did not know her father. Along with her young brother and the one-day-old baby, she was left in the hands of an aging grandmother who had very little to offer them.

They had been living a life of abject poverty for about two years when I heard their story as I interacted with the people of Inyaanzani village. It was my habit to enquire about people and how they lived. I was told about Mercy's family and how she and her two siblings led a miserable life with their aged grandmother. With their grandmother's permission, I immediately took all three children to MCF Ndalani. Here they received food and accommodation and were able to attend school.

Mercy knew that her mother had died because no medical expert was available to help her deliver safely. She knew that if a doctor had been present, her mother's life could have been saved. She knew she was an orphan because of a lack of medical experts in their village. One day, she shared her future aspirations with me. She was in class 3. She told me, "Daddy, I want to be a doctor in the future to save the lives of others."

I found this to be a very powerful prayer from a child who aspired to save lives by serving as a doctor. She desired that no else endure what happened to her mother and family. She wanted to be able to make a difference in people's lives. I took her aspirations seriously and kept on monitoring her performance in class. I received a good report that she was doing very well in sciences.

She completed form 4 (grade 12) in MCF Secondary School and attained a mean grade of B+. This was enough to enable her to pursue her career dream of being a doctor. I eventually secured her acceptance at the University of Nairobi, and she earned a bachelor's degree in medicine and surgery. Mercy graduated in December 2013 and became the first medical doctor from the Inyaanzani area.

As I reflect on Mercy's life I see how God has not only transformed her life but also gave her a desire to serve others. She understood why her mother had died, and this inspired her to become a medical doctor. God used the difficulties in her life to give her the heart to serve others in His Name. With God, nothing is wasted. With God, nothing is by acci-⚡ dent. With God, no suffering is pointless.

In our rehabilitation work, we have listened to many moving stories from suffering children. One case was Elizabeth. In 1995, she was barely six years old when both her parents were taken to hospital in Eldoret in critical condition. Elizabeth was left alone at home, with no one to take care of her. That night she was attacked and sexually harassed by unknown persons.

The police who were on patrol took her to the police station, where she was given some temporary shelter and protection. While in police custody, her parents succumbed to their illness and died. Elizabeth stayed at the police station for three days waiting for someone, a relative or even a family friend, to come and get her, but no one came. The police wanted a quick fix to her case, so they moved her to a juvenile remand prison.

This was a correctional home for children with wayward behaviour. The children were mostly beaten and harassed by the authorities and fellow children. Elizabeth, by virtue of being here, was also treated and punished like a wayward child and given corporal punishment every day.

Life for Elizabeth was unbearable. Being so young, she could hardly understand the environment around her. She was weak and fragile. There was never enough to eat. The older boys would scramble for food all the time, and she would miss out. The rule in prison was survival of the fittest.

She slept on three pieces of wood bound together on both sides by metal bars. There was no mattress. She only had a blanket that she shared with three other children. The guards woke them up periodically to take a roll call. The place had a high wall and a barbed wire fence with piercing sharp ends at the top to ensure no one would jump outside. Furthermore, the dogs outside the fence were trained to devour anything that moved at night. This made escape impossible. But all the same, a roll call was mandatory, and not just one—sometimes two or three per night.

How can God let this happen to me? Doesn't He know I was too young to be orphaned when He took my parents? Does He hear my prayers? These questions plagued her mind, and she would cry bitterly.

How is it possible that the whole world would conspire against me to make me suffer? Doesn't anyone care anymore? she asked herself. She believed that the world was full of evil people. This made her develop a combination of fear of and hatred for others.

I saw her one day when I went to preach in the prison. I remember looking into her eyes, and she looked back at me. I called her to step forward and held her close to me. She was too young to be in this rough place. She was dirty, smelling of urine, and had dried porridge from breakfast all over her face. When it was time to leave, I went to the office and asked why the small child was in prison.

I learned that her parents had died and her immediate family members could not be traced. In other words, she was here to be protected from the potential dangers she would have faced out there. It was ironic that the so-called "protection from danger" was more traumatizing than being left alone on the streets.

As I went back home, my heart was filled with thoughts of remorse about the little girl I had just seen. I felt that she was too young and too innocent to be in such a place.

Several days later, I came back to the prison and took little Elizabeth with me to MCF Eldoret. She was excited to be part of a family where she was treated with love and care, given food, prayed for, taken to school and given a good place to sleep. Unlike in the prison, where she was bullied, shouted at and ordered around, at MCF she met new brothers and sisters with whom she could sing, play and pray. They shared food with love, and not by grabbing everything from others, as was the case in prison. My wife, Esther, was very instrumental in showing motherly love to Elizabeth and other young ones that I had brought to MCF.

Personally, I spent a lot of time with Elizabeth, counselling her and trying to help her build a positive attitude in life. She looked at the world as a place full of savages. She liked keeping a distance and not sharing a lot with others. She would shrink away whenever someone came close to her. But we kept showing her the good side of life and some of the good people in life. Even the stories we told her were of good people who played the role of heroes in other people's lives. Slowly, Elizabeth started trusting and accepting the people around her.

She studied in MCF Ndalani right from nursery to form 4. She passed her KCSE exams and qualified to join the University of Nairobi. In 2013, Elizabeth graduated with a bachelor's degree in nursing.

In my MCF mission, I have encountered stubborn children and children who were rooted in drug abuse—children who are very difficult to rehabilitate. But the more they disturbed me, the more they dissented, the more I persisted, until they changed from their wayward ways. Having decided to work with street children, I was prepared to handle and transform difficult cases. I have been very patient because I believe that God sent them to me for a purpose. I hardly know the language of defeat, and I have never believed that there are things impossible to accomplish in this world. Likewise, there are no difficult people who cannot change. I used to tell myself that if Saul changed from his callous ways and became Paul, embracing Christianity and preaching the gospel of Jesus, then anybody could change.

The depth and extent of internal and external pain that so many children live with on a daily basis is unimaginable. I would not have been able to handle this work of rescuing children unless God had given me great psychological strength each step along the way. I have complete empathy with the children because I, too, have been beaten, abandoned and forgotten. At the same time, God has sustained me so that I have not been overcome by the suffering. I rely on Almighty God through much prayer, and He enables me to have confidence in Him with a hopeful and positive attitude in the midst of so many challenges. I continually remind myself that this is God's work and I am His representative.

It continually amazes me how light this massive burden is when it is carried by Almighty God. Truly, this work is impossible for any one man to do. His yoke is easy, and His burden is light.

And it is this truth, this desire to trust God with all my heart, that I seek to instill in MCF. I do not hide struggles from my children. Why would I prevent them from seeing Almighty God work miracles? In fact, it is the very exposure of the children to a miracle-working God that enables them to grow in their faith. We invite the entire MCF fraternity to come together and pray. We have done so for the provision of clean water, for the government to grant us a permit to have a school, for wisdom in helping our fellow Kenyans. The children have experienced God first-hand. In this way the stories of the Bible come alive because the children can relate to characters in the Bible who also experienced God first-hand.

Yes, there is much suffering. And while it appears that the mystery of suffering in the world is not compatible with an Almighty God, our faith in Him has proven time after time that God does work all things, including suffering, together for good when we believe on His name.

Joseph, popularly known as "Njoro," was one of the most difficult children I ever brought to MCF. He joined with the pioneer group in the early '90s. He had lived in the streets of Eldoret for a long time, and when I took him to MCF, he failed to shed off the negative behaviours of a street child. He continued abusing drugs, escaping from the centre until even I lost count of the number of times he escaped, stole and fought fellow children and staff. Once I was visited by someone who ran a street children's home in Eldoret where Njoro had once been taken but was expelled after a short while. This man told me, "Don't keep this boy Njoro around here. He is like a rotten egg that spoils all your eggs."

Njoro had a difficult beginning. He was born in the Kamukunji slums of Eldoret in 1981. His mother sold local brew and was a drunken woman. Sometimes she would get drunk early in the morning and sleep the whole day as her children cried for food. The people she sold beer to sometimes snuck away without paying. And sometimes when she had no food, she gave her children beer to drink so that they could fall asleep and stop disturbing her. Fighting was the order of the day in their household because of the disorderly nature of the ever-present drunkards.

In his early childhood Njoro led the life of a street child. At the very least, he had a place to call home. During the day he would go out and beg for food in the streets and rummage in the garbage bins, and in the evening he would return home to sleep. In 1988, when he was seven years old, he moved from Kamukunji and became a full-time street child in Eldorettown. He joined a group that operated from an alley on Oloo Street next to the Eldoret market. Those days, the level of crime being perpetuated by the street children was high, and Njoro got arrested many times—whenever the police conducted swoops in the streets. The police rarely took the street children to court. They would only beat them, scare them and release them back to the streets. Out of fear, Njoro would relocate to estates such as Munyaka and Langas and only come back to town when the swoops had decreased.

Njoro had a small body frame, and so he was trained in pickpocketing by the bigger street boys. He would enter a stall in the market and steal from the trader while hiding under the table or squeezing himself in a corner. The loot was then shared with the big boys.

One day, the big boys plotted to steal from one of the local shops at night when the owner had gone home. As a good student of crime, Njoro was the one they used to accomplish their mission. They placed him in a box and sealed it. They approached the shop owner and asked him to keep the box for them and they would collect it the following day. The businessman obliged without questioning the contents of the box.

At night, Njoro was able to cut through the box from inside using a razor blade. He got out, took an empty sack, and bundled in a number of electronics, including cameras, radios, watches and flashlights. He managed to open the window from inside, and the big boys took off with the loot.

Life on the streets was never easy for Njoro or other children. Children would steal from the street vendors and if caught would be severely beaten. Or worse. A child was once caught stealing money from a businessman in the market. The boy had allegedly grabbed a purse containing the daily collections from one of the traders. As he tried to get away he was cornered and beaten to death.

Even when the street children were successful in stealing and escaping the businessmen, they would disagree on how to share the stolen items of food, merchandise or money and would fight and injure each another.

One evening as I visited the street children, I heard that some of them had been badly beaten in the market after getting caught stealing earlier that day. I found them crammed by the fire, nursing serious injuries. I noticed that one of them was so small. His lips and eyes were swollen, and he had a cut on his forehead. The boy was crying in pain. I tried to touch his face to examine the extent of the injuries, but he slapped my hand in bitterness. Perhaps he thought I was one of the common assailants in the streets who just wanted to laugh at him. I had never met him before. The children who were friendly to me said he was new to their camp. I gave him a packet of milk and bread. He gulped down the food and then looked at me in a friendly manner.

"What is your name?" I asked him.

He answered without hesitation, "I'm called Njoro."

"Where did you come from?" I asked further.

"We used to live in Kamukunji, but my mother left; I don't know where she went."

I kept wanting to know more about him. "Where have you been staying?"

He answered, "In an alley next to the bus park."

That evening I took some children with me to my house in Pioneer Estate; the little injured Njoro was one of them.

He stayed with us and the many other children that I had already brought into MCF. My wife, Esther, nursed his wounds. She washed them, bandaged them and applied some ointment, and the boy slowly recovered. By the time I took him in, Njoro had lived on the streets of Eldoret since he last escaped from his drunken mother five years earlier.

He also had a brother and small sister, but he had no idea where they had gone. Theirs was a broken family, and everyone was on their own.

After he had stayed with us for about two months, I came back one evening and my wife informed me that Njoro was missing. Right away I knew that he had gone back to the streets. I went back to town the following day, and while walking along Oloo Street, near the market, I spotted Njoro with some other street children, standing outside a hotel that was known as Lengut. I called him, and he came to me running. "Let's go back home," I told him. He did not resist. I held his hand as we walked to the car, and I drove him back to my house in Pioneer.

About a year later, I relocated all the children from Eldoret to Ndalani. Njoro managed to escape and remain behind. He never wanted to leave Eldoret town. About six months after I had settled the others in Ndalani, I went back to Eldoret. While I was running errands, I found Njoro idling on Oloo Street. He was hungry and dirty. He looked sad and worried. I think he had been fighting.

We were happy to see each other again. I gave him food. I told him he was still my son. I said I still wanted him back. Every child needs this reassurance. I asked him to go with me to Ndalani. This time around, he agreed. We travelled on the long journey to Ndalani. Together.

Even though I thought Ndalani would be difficult for him to escape from, Njoro always found a way of getting out. He snuck out on several occasions and went to Thika town, where he reverted to sniffing glue and abusing drugs. He would sneak out of the centre at 2 a.m. when others were asleep. It was difficult to lock him down.

In 2000, while he was in form 3, Njoro escaped again and went all the way to Nairobi. He was addicted to street life and always felt like a fish out of water whenever he was not on the streets. While in the city he attempted to snatch a purse from a passerby at a busy bus park known as Nyama-kima. In the process, he was caught, beaten and arrested by the police. While being interrogated, he told them he was from the Mully Children's Family. We later received notice that he had been put in remand. I sent one of my staff to inform the authorities that Njoro was a former street boy undergoing rehabilitation at MCF. They agreed to release him, and he was brought back to Ndalani.

Everybody around me had the idea that Njoro was impossible to rehabilitate. Many people in MCF felt that it was time to show Njoro the exit door. All the teaching staff, whom Njoro had been upsetting in class, were in agreement that this was a case of someone who would never change. At one point he became so difficult to contain that the staff recommended that I expel him. His letter of expulsion was written and brought to me for signing, but I shelved the idea.

I was not in a hurry to make such decisions. I chose not to condemn him but rather to understand him. I knew his family had broken up, and perhaps he was hurting inside, his solace being to engage in drug abuse. Perhaps he was feeling that nothing in the world mattered.

Even after he kept committing one mistake after another, I kept giving him a second chance to reform because I believed that MCF was established to change lives and that we should not get defeated in doing so. Still, the bad reports kept coming in. Njoro has stolen. Njoro fought in class. Njoro has been aggravating other children. Njoro refused to attend devotion services. Njoro has run away from the centre.

One day I called him to sit with me under a tree in Ndalani, where I talked to him for about three hours. It was the longest session I ever had with a single child. I shared with him the story of the prodigal son and told him not to blow away a unique opportunity for transforming his life for the better. I reiterated to him that there was nothing pleasurable in smoking marijuana and stealing. There was nothing to gain in fighting with his fellow brothers and sisters and causing unnecessary confrontations with teachers. I told him that God had better things in store for him. I could see a tear roll down his cheek. I advised him to re-examine himself and what he wanted to be in the future. I told him that many people are hurting in this world—having lost loved ones, property or inheritance—but they accept their fate and move on. I told him that he had two options: to stay in MCF and build a better future for himself or go back to the streets and be doomed. He promised to change and follow the rules and regulations laid down in MCF.

After that talk, Njoro was able to settle down, and he managed to complete his secondary education at MCF Ndalani in 2001, receiving a C in KCSE. Judging from his troubled past, this was a good grade. We celebrated him. In 2003, I enrolled him at the Rift Valley Technical Training Institute (RVTTI) in Eldoret for a diploma course in mechanical engineering. He graduated in 2005. While at RVTTI, Njoro came and delivered good news to us: "Daddy, I'm now saved; the Lord is my personal saviour." He even came back and preached to us in Ndalani, and we all thanked God for powerfully transforming this man's life. Njoro later became the Christian Union (CU) Chairman in RVTTI. This was the greatest breakthrough I ever witnessed among the MCF children.

In 2007, Njoro was offered a job with an engineering company in
Nairobi. He later worked with another company. In 2012 he left to begin
a children's home in Ngong (Kajiado). By 2015, he had already rescued
over 80 street children.

When we celebrated MCF's 25 years of existence, Njoro came
back to give his testimony. He described MCF as a place full of love and
patience. His story is a living testimony that God can change people. It
tells us that it does not matter where we came from and what we did in
the past, but the most important thing is where we are heading.

Njoro later revealed to me that he decided to help street children
because he succeeded in life as a result of other people's love and
patience for him. He acknowledged that street children could misbe-
have but added that it is important for everyone not to give up on them.
"Daddy, sometimes I wonder what would have happened to me if you
decided to give up on me. What would I have become?" he once posed
to me. It was a very emotional question.

I'm glad Njoro dedicated his life to Christ and is now one of the
active soldiers of the Lord here on earth. He is an embodiment of the
biblical saying "the stone the builders rejected has become the cornerstone" (Matthew 21:42). Njoro had been rejected and hated by many
people because of his abrasive, stubborn and uncontrollable nature. But
today he is a pillar of society. Many children depend on him.

Every morning, his children recite a prayer:

> I have lived with rejection all my life, braving cold nights in the streets. I
> have faced hard-hearted people who refused to give me food and care
> when I begged but showed me their wrath when I stole to survive. I have
> scars on my face and bruises in my heart, the sort of a person that no
> one can love.
>
> Now, Lord, I ask You to heal my heart so that the experience of those
> cold nights will teach me to be concerned about others. Let my rejection and
> abandonment teach me to be close to others in their loneliness. Amen.

❄ ❄ ❄

Yes, there is great suffering, and the plight of the street children is
deplorable. But we also know that God is at work in mighty ways among
the children. Each child who has come to MCF has a personal and powerful testimony of God's grace. As their lives are transformed, they are
able to encounter God in a new way. I have shared only a few stories
from the thousands of lives that MCF has touched. But these stories

reveal how God is accomplishing His purpose in my life, and He is accomplishing His purposes in each of my children's lives. He rescued Georgo, Kariuki, Wilson, Mercy, Elizabeth and Njoro, and each has been given a specific gift in their understanding of God and His mercy. And it is this personal touch that God has in each person's life that enables them to willingly serve others with a genuine heart of love.

Chapter Seven
DON'T PRAISE ME; PRAISE GOD!

Since establishing MCF in November 1989 I have been able to help many people and positively impact thousands of lives. I have participated in saving the lives of children who were on the verge of dying and provided shelter to people who had no place to call home. I helped restore the dreams of hopeless children. I also helped establish schools, pay fees, build capacity for neglected men and women, provide food for hungry families and create employment for hundreds of residents around MCF.

The feedback from all these forms of assistance has been amazing. People have written letters, shared testimonies in churches and spoken about me as an extraordinary human being. It is good to appreciate what has been done to you, but some of the beneficiaries go to the extent of portraying Charles Mulli as super-human. Even visitors who come to our centres and stand in awe of the activities of MCF find it difficult to believe that this organization was established, managed and developed by an ordinary Kenyan. They end up praising and thanking me too much.

Amid all the praise, I choose to remain calm and resist the temptation to believe that the philanthropic gestures I extend to MCF beneficiaries are of my own volition. I resist the temptation to take glory for the success of MCF. God uses me to take on a marvellous work, but this is God's work, not mine. I am only His servant, and so the credit goes squarely to Him. In my interactions with friends and members of the public I keep reiterating that MCF is God's idea—that it was given to me as a vision to help street children and that I succeed only by God's miracles and power of providence.

Sometimes I look at what MCF has accomplished and I am amazed. I just cannot tell how it happened. The assistance that many people have received through MCF is not mine at all; it's God's assistance. The love that we show the MCF children is not our love; it's God's love. As ordinary human beings, we become tired as we press on to help people whom we are not related to biologically. Our work involves long days and many trying situations. Every family is a 24/7 operation, and ours is no different. It is only through God that I was able to bring in thousands of children and call them mine.

Some people wonder, does this man really love all these children as if they were his own? And all I can say is that yes, it is true. In my heart I love them as my very own. That is what they are. As it says in 1 John 3:1, "See what great love the Father has lavished on us, that we should be called children of God! And that is what we are!" All of us were born into sin and were separated from God. But the blood of Jesus has made it possible for anyone who puts their faith in Jesus to become a child of God. I put my faith in Jesus, and God has brought me into His family as a total child of His. I am not partially God's child. I am totally and completely His, because of His great love. And this same great love that God my Father has for me He poured into my heart to be an earthly father to all these children. This enables me to point them to their heavenly Father. When I go to God in prayer, I tell Him that His mercy and love have enabled thousands of abandoned children to feel part of a family again.

The Almighty God chose to use me to reach out to His people and touch them where they were hurting most. That is why I have maintained that beneficiaries and other people who applaud what MCF is accomplishing should thank God and not me.

Because I have always known that MCF was God's work, I did not boast about our achievements in public for the first ten years. The centre remained unknown, quietly impacting thousands of lives. Many people did not realize what we were doing, but I was happy simply to know that God was using MCF to bring hope to destitute children. The results were positive, and I did everything not for personal glory but for the fulfillment of God's will.

In other words, we gave assistance with the right hand but did not allow the left hand to know what was happening. I did not call the press to witness what I was doing, because I knew the Person to whom I was accountable had already seen what was happening, and

He was pleased with the good work we were doing. As long as God's will to help the needy was achieved, the rest did not matter. I did not brag or seek to show people that I was the super-hero in the children's lives.

I have a friend who was so impressed by the work of MCF that he wrote an email asking to support some of the projects we were undertaking. After several weeks of exchanging emails with me, he opted to support one of the sustainability projects. He was delighted about what we were doing and chose to boost our income. When he later visited Kenya to see the project, his words were amazing. He said, "I'm so happy for this chance to meet you, Charles. It is even better than meeting the pope. I cannot find a person to compare with you."

Even though this statement seemed like a deep expression of his excitement and appreciation of the work we were doing, I felt like he represented a majority of the people who constantly praised and thanked me as the individual responsible for the success of MCF.

I received his accolades positively but responded to him simply: "This is all the work of God. He is the one who is worthy of the praise. Human beings like me do not have the capacity to undertake and sustain such a massive initiative."

It is said that when you put a lot of pressure into a balloon, it grows big and flies really high, but a slight touch on it will cause a huge burst, and it will fall back to the ground in pieces. This is food for thought. Sometimes when people are praised a lot they develop a high sense of self-importance; they begin walking up in the sky. In the process, they will be preparing themselves for a massive downfall.

In our normal lives, many people amass too much credit for their achievements and get so self-centred about themselves. They brag about what they own and what they have accomplished. Such people take offence when they are not appreciated in the right way or when they are not addressed appropriately with their big titles or when they are not awarded a medal. They always want to be honoured and appreciated wherever they go. They are quick to recount their success story to whoever cares to listen. They say nothing about God and are not willing to share whatever they have with the needy. Just like the balloon, they are inflated and are flying high. However, it takes only a slight knock for them to come tumbling back to earth.

As the Bible says in Matthew 6:1–4,

"Be careful not to practice your righteousness in front of others to be seen by them. If you do, you will have no reward from your Father in heaven. So when you give to the needy, do not announce it with trumpets, as the hypocrites do in the synagogues and on the streets, to be honored by others. Truly I tell you, they have received their reward in full. But when you give to the needy, do not let your left hand know what your right hand is doing, so that your giving may be in secret. Then your Father, who sees what is done in secret, will reward you."

In Luke 18:10–14, Jesus tells a parable warning against self-praise, judging others and developing feelings of righteousness:

"Two men went up to the temple to pray, one a Pharisee and the other a tax collector. The Pharisee stood by himself and prayed: 'God, I thank you that I am not like other people—robbers, evildoers, adulterers—or even like this tax collector. I fast twice a week and give a tenth of all I get.' But the tax collector stood at a distance. He would not even look up to heaven, but beat his breast and said, 'God, have mercy on me, a sinner.'" [Then Jesus said,] "I tell you that this man, rather than the other, went home justified before God. For all those who exalt themselves will be humbled, and those who humble themselves will be exalted."

These verses are an encouragement to me and a reminder that it is God who is at work. As I humble myself daily and rely on His power moment by moment, He works in me and through me to accomplish His purposes. The result is that I get to look at all that has happened at MCF and in my heart I know God has done it all. I can marvel at how amazing He is and that He even used a person like me.

When we first began our ministry, people did not understand the importance of what we were doing. Few people paid any attention. However, as I continued to serve God in the field of the less fortunate, opportunities continued to arise to share with others about the work. As the work began to expand in a more diversified way, more people came to see what we were doing. And the media became more and more interested in the vision of MCF.

On November 13, 2014, I was invited by TV host David Makali to the Citizen TV morning talk show. It was on the eve of the silver jubilee celebrations. We were discussing 25 years of MCF. I told the viewers how I received a call from God and abandoned all my business ventures in order to engage in rescuing street children and other vulnerable

groups in the society. I shared the testimony of how God had been faithful to us—how we started with three children in 1989, grew to 300 by
1995 and cared for over 2,000 children by 2014. Within the same
period we had managed to open other centres in Mombasa, Kitale,
Lodwar, Kampala and Dar es Salaam.

The response from the viewers was overwhelming. I give glory to
God for all the sentiments that were expressed, which included,

"Dr. Mulli, thanks for pursuing your purpose; you have encouraged this
country to know there are faithful men out there who can be good stew-
ards over what God has given us."

"That's great work there, Dr. Mulli; you are walking in the footsteps of
Jesus Christ Himself."

"Dr. Mulli is a true servant of Jesus Christ. I will try and give back to the
society at least a fraction...Thanks for teaching me that humility is key."

"These are our true heroes. Why are they never recognized or even
decorated?"

"Dr. Mulli has given me the greatest gift in recent times. If we all had such
a big heart, we would be the most blessed country in the world."

"Dr. Mulli, if we had 1 of you for every 100 politicians, Kenya would sur-
pass Vision 2030 by 2020."

"This interview is making me cry. What a heart! This is what Kenya needs."

"Morning, Doctor Mulli; what you are doing is beyond human. God bless
you, but why don't you start one in Kisumu?"

"If Dr. Mulli can do all these with his personal resources, then how much
can national resources do?"

"Dr. Mulli's farming exploits in the arid lands of Yatta is an amazing case
study that shows we can defeat hunger."

"Congrats, Dr. Mulli. Kindly bring your branch to Migori county. I like your
work. Be blessed."

The comments people made about national development showed
their frustration and disillusionment with mere talk from political leaders and government officials. They were not interested in rhetoric.
They were interested in actions. It was clear that we needed to take
action to end suffering and hopelessness among the people. We
needed to end child neglect, abuse, exploitation, defilement, child
labour and many other unfortunate occurrences. I realized that the
Kenyan society was lacking role models who inspired people to feel

proud to be Kenyan. I saw a society that desperately needed people who could make a difference.

In the Sermon on the Mount, Jesus says,

 "You are the light of the world. A city set on a hill cannot be hidden, nor do people light a lamp and put it under a basket, but on a stand and it gives light to all in the house. In the same way, let your light shine before others, so that they may see your good works and give glory to your Father who is in heaven."

Our work at MCF from the beginning was always open for people to see. But God, in His timing and in His way, began to instill in more and more people a curiosity about our work. They began to seek us out to learn about what was happening at MCF. And it was my joy to share with them about what God was doing.

After listening to the comments of viewers in response to the works of MCF, I realized that people were not simply praising me but were inspired by what I was doing. Their first reaction was one of surprise—they felt that no person could make such a difference. But then some began to ask themselves the question "What can I do?" I then realized that I needed to share what God was doing through me in order to inspire others. Obedience and faith are inspirational. Deep in our hearts we want to be part of God's plan. And when people saw that I had stepped out in faith, they too believed they could step out as well in what God had called them to do.

I believe that the ultimate purpose of our living on earth is to serve the Lord, our Master. That means we are not the masters ourselves, but we are servants of the Master. Servants agree to be used by the master in whatever way. Servants acknowledge that they are only representatives of the master. This also implies that even what we own is basically not our possession but rather God's possession that He is simply keeping in our hands, to hold on His behalf and use to serve His people.

The Lord expects us as true servants of God not to do anything from selfish ambition or from a cheap desire to boast but to be humble towards each other, never thinking we are better than others, and to look out for each other's interests, not just for our own.

Jesus taught His disciples to humble themselves and serve the people selflessly. Give to all and serve all. As John 13:12–17 says,

> When Jesus had finished washing their feet, he put on his clothes and returned to his place. "Do you understand what I have done for you?" he asked them. "You call me 'Teacher' and 'Lord,' and rightly so, for that is what I am. Now that I, your Lord and Teacher, have washed your feet, you also should wash one another's feet. I have set you an example that you should do as I have done for you. Very truly I tell you, no servant is greater than his master, nor is a messenger greater than the one who sent him. Now that you know these things, you will be blessed if you do them."

There are dozens of passages in the Bible that talk about serving God. First Samuel 12:24 says, "Be sure to fear the LORD and serve him faithfully with all your heart." Colossians 3:23–24 says, "Whatever you do, work at it with all your heart, as working for the Lord, not for human masters, since you know that you will receive an inheritance from the Lord as a reward."

But how do we serve God? Many people have often mistaken going to church, singing in the choir, praying and praising God's name as the ultimate way of serving Him. It's important to engage in all of the these, but God looks more at what we do than at what we say (or pretend to do). Galatians 5:13 says, "You, my brothers and sisters, were called to be free. But do not use your freedom to indulge the flesh; rather, serve one another humbly in love." And Matthew 25:40 declares, "Whatever you did for one of the least of these brothers and sisters of mine, you did for me."

I'm strongly impressed by 1 Peter 4:10–11:

> Each of you should use whatever gift you have received to serve others, as faithful stewards of God's grace in its various forms. If anyone speaks, they should do so as one who speaks the very words of God. If anyone serves, they should do so with the strength God provides, so that in all things God may be praised through Jesus Christ.

Peter makes it clear that we have received our gifts from God for two purposes—to serve others and to bring praise to God. Serving isn't about us receiving attention or glory; it is for Him to receive glory.

Personally, I believe that God owns all that we possess, but as His servants our work is to distribute His wealth among the poor. We give to the poor to glorify God. When we fail to help the poor, God is not impressed, because we are attempting to block His love from reaching to the poor. He will instead put you aside, recover His wealth from you and use someone else to distribute it to the poor. And if you honour Him and serve the poor on His behalf, God will give you more in abundance.

The story of the late Mobutu Sese Seko, the former president of Zaire (now Democratic Republic of Congo), is a tragic example of the vanity behind amassing too much wealth by hook and by crook. During his leadership, people were afraid of mentioning him by name. He was referred to as "Lion Warrior," "Saviour of the Nation" and "Supreme Combatant," among other extraordinary adjectives. His full name was Mobutu Sese Seko Kuku Ngbendu Wa Zabanga, translated as "The Warrior Who Knows No Defeat Because Of His Endurance And Inflexible Will And Is All Powerful, Leaving Fire In His Wake As He Goes From Conquest To Conquest."

He became president in 1965. He amassed too much wealth at the expense of his suffering people, and by 1985, he was worth about five billion US dollars. Unfortunately, all this wealth was from looting and lack of compassion for the poor, not from hard work. This was a rich country full of minerals, but the president grabbed everything for himself. He lived a lavish and luxurious life that few people in the world could afford; even well-to-do business magnates in the developed world could not compare to him. Literally, he owned everything in his country while his citizens remained the poorest people in the world. He knew nothing about sharing with them and coming down to lift them up. In fact, he stole from them and further pushed the Congolese people into poverty and dejection. He was deposed in 1997 after 32 years of power.

Leaders are from God. They rule the people on behalf of God, and I believe God had given Mobutu the authority to rule Zaire, but he failed to uphold the dignity of the people, develop them, guarantee them a good future and bring them closer to God. That is the kind of leadership that Almighty God expects from rulers. Mobutu was only concerned about himself and his selfish interests, against God's command that requires us to be our brother's keeper.

God expects leaders to show love to their subjects, give them guidance and make a positive difference in their lives. God has bestowed a lot of wealth to us on earth, and He expects the leaders to fairly and truthfully preside over an equitable sharing process that makes everyone feel part and parcel of the nation. God does not expect one person to grab everything and run away as others wallow in abject poverty. Just like Mahatma Gandhi once said, "The world has enough for everybody's need, but not enough for everyone's greed."

A major element of being a humble leader is prayer. To pray is to confess to God our inability to accomplish anything on our own and places the focus on Him. I have seen many answers to prayer at MCF. On several occasions, I have received numerous calls from people who are in dire need of assistance. I get messages from people asking for assistance from MCF who seem to be desperately hanging on in life. In such cases, I pray for the person—even through the phone—and advise them to continue trusting God to perform miracles. I tell them that everything is possible with God. After listening to their sorrows, I comfort them and cast their sorrows onto Him who cares. I pray and allow God to do as His wishes. These prayers have always been answered, and many needy people have ended up seeing God perform what they considered impossible in their lives.

In most cases, after we pray, God uses us to reach out to such needy people and rescue them, or He simply opens up other avenues to enable us to alleviate the suffering of those people. And whatever channel God uses, the outcome has always been positive and promising.

What often gives me a lot of satisfaction is seeing a positive change in the lives of people. When we restore hope to the hopeless, I get very excited. I get the feeling and satisfaction of an achiever. When we pray for the sick and they are healed, I become so touched and humbled. When abandoned children are able to pursue an education and emerge successful in life, I get excited.

When I see a soul that was deeply rooted in sinful ways being restored back to God, I jubilate. I get excited about the positive impact in people's lives because this forms the basis of a good and prosperous society. Most importantly, this is what God truly desires for humanity. As the Bible says in 1 Timothy 2:4, God "wants all people to be saved and to come to a knowledge of the truth."

I especially like this verse because it uses the words "all people." It does not say "some people." It does not put a certain group above others. It simply means everybody. Whether you are a king, an ordinary citizen or a street child, the Lord desires that you will know the truth and be saved. Thus those who teach the Word of God and those who are ready to be used by God must reach out to everybody without discrimination. We should not only pray and fellowship with the rich who can give handsome tithes, but we should also go down and fellowship with the poor who have nothing to offer. They are people of God, and He needs them to be saved too.

Besides the material assistance that we have extended to many people through MCF, I have been able to stand with many people in prayer, especially as they went through some of the most difficult moments of their lives. This is what I consider the most important aspect of my calling.

Another key aspect to humility is to remember that we are called to serve. It gives me pleasure to serve fellow human beings and be able to be used by God to impact lives positively. Even in my normal conversations with brethren and ministers of the gospel, I always insist that serving God is all about serving humanity. I advocate doing good to humanity as our main preoccupation as co-workers of Jesus Christ.

In this context my favourite passage has been the parable of the Good Samaritan in Luke 10:30–34. Jesus says,

> "A man was going down from Jerusalem to Jericho, when he was attacked by robbers. They stripped him of his clothes, beat him and went away, leaving him half dead. A priest happened to be going down the same road, and when he saw the man, he passed by on the other side. So too, a Levite, when he came to the place and saw him, passed by on the other side. But a Samaritan, as he traveled, came where the man was; and when he saw him, he took pity on him. He went to him and bandaged his wounds, pouring on oil and wine. Then he put the man on his own donkey, brought him to an inn and took care of him."

This teaching calls us to exercise kindness and love for others. It calls us to take other people's problems as our problems. It calls us to carry out the good deeds of God and not simply worship Him with our lips.

This is the theme in 1 John 2:3–11 as well:

> We know that we have come to know him if we keep his commands. Whoever says, "I know him," but does not do what he commands is a liar, and the truth is not in that person. But if anyone obeys his word, love for God is truly made complete in them. This is how we know we are in him: Whoever claims to live in him must live as Jesus did. Dear friends, I am not writing you a new command but an old one, which you have had since the beginning. This old command is the message you have heard. Yet I am writing you a new command; its truth is seen in him and in you, because the darkness is passing and the true light is already shining.

Anyone who claims to be in the light but hates a brother or sister is still in the darkness. Anyone who loves their brother and sister lives in the light, and there is nothing in them to make them stumble. But anyone who hates a brother or sister is in the darkness and walks around in the darkness. They do not know where they are going, because the darkness has blinded them.

Ultimately, as Jesus says in Matthew 25:40, "The King will reply, '...whatever you did for one of the least of these brothers and sisters of mine, you did for me.'"

Love is unending. The love that we show other people will carry on after we die. Jesus will reveal what we did for others in the life to come. This is the secret for people who help the poor. These people don't feel bothered. They don't feel like they are doing too much. They don't worry about their reward. Instead, they are looking forward to their eternal reward.

Some people have only a short-term reward here on earth. But we look for the long-term reward. So it is never a burden to help the poor. It is a privilege. It is an honour.

It is a calling.

Chapter Eight
A MISSION TO REACH CHILDREN WITH THE GOOD NEWS OF JESUS

When God put His love into my heart, it came with a passion to fulfill God's purpose for humanity. In Acts, we read how Jesus sent His disciples to be His witnesses in Jerusalem, in all Judea and Samaria and to the uttermost parts of the earth and to make disciples of all nations, baptizing them in the name of the Father, the Son and the Holy Spirit and teaching them to obey everything Jesus commanded.

These instructions from Jesus to the disciples form the motivation for my ministry. There is an urgency in my heart to be used by God to take His message wherever He wants me to go. As we brought the Good News of Jesus to children, God expanded our ministry to meet their needs in many ways.

MCF started by taking the gospel to the streets to reach children with the Good News about Jesus Christ. We preached in slums and wanted to give our love and our passion to people. We wanted not simply to look into their faces but to feel with them. To pray with them. To encourage them. We prayed for the sick. We provided food for the poor. We reached out the way we were commanded to by Jesus Christ, meeting both physical and spiritual needs.

After establishing MCF, I visited many parts of Kenya to assess the plight of street children and to fellowship with brothers and sisters across the nation. On my trips, I travelled to Kisumu, Nakuru, Kajiado, Mombasa, Kakamega, Kitale, Kapenguria and many other urban centres. While in these places, I mainly visited slums, villages and other lowly places in order to encourage the poor people not to give up but to depend on God to change their fortunes in life.

With my MCF staff and prayer friends, I took evangelism to the people who thought that God had forgotten them. My message to the people was "God is always with you, even in your lowest moments." We donated some food to them and encouraged them to keep trusting God. Even though I had brought thousands of children to MCF, I kept encountering very many needy children, and I thought of ways of helping them.

In Kitale, we toured some of the slums where poor people lived. We went to the Kipsongo slums and gained first-hand experience of how people were leading deplorable lives. Children were crying for food, but there was nothing to eat. The place was mainly inhabited by poor, landless people from the Turkana community who moved to Kitale in search of jobs as farm workers, cattle herders and home guards.

Some of these people would go for days without food. Many adults had died from HIV/AIDS and other diseases that were prevalent in the slums, and they left behind children who could not support themselves. Most of these children were malnourished and sickly; their "employment" was roaming Kitale town begging for food. At some point while preaching in Kipsongo, I looked at the crowd and saw over 1,000 children who needed to be rescued and helped. We took several of them to MCF, but the demand was extremely high. I prayed to God to give me the strength and the resources to do something substantial for the people of Kipsongo.

There was a tremendous need in all age groups. Yet because I focused on children, I decided to open a feeding centre in the Kipsongo slums to provide needy children with food and education during the day. The children would return to their homes in the evening because we could not afford to provide full-time accommodation for them. However, the little we did brought together a majority of the slum children for fellowship and also gave them an opportunity to learn and appreciate the Word of God. This at least stopped the children from roaming all over the town begging for food. By 2015, our centre was catering for more than 400 children.

One of the children we rescued from Kipsongo was a gang leader in his early twenties named John. He was too old to come to MCF Eldoret, and so I often met him in the street and took food for him. He had never been to school, so I taught him to read in the slums. God really worked in his heart and mind, because he later became a teacher and then went on to become an evangelist and preacher at MCF Kipsongo. This showed me how God really does the impossible, even if we think it is too late. He can take an illiterate person who seems like a lost cause and not worth investing time into and turn him into a powerful tool for the gospel.

In one of my trips to Mombasa in 2003, I met brothers and sisters who told me about the poor children in that area who had resorted to work as beach boys to earn a living. Their jobs were not well-defined. They simply did anything and everything they could to survive, like carrying goods and accompanying people to the ocean. As we were chatting, I was approached by a man who told me he was selling a property located in Vipingo, Kilifi. He had built a private academy but closed it when all the children dropped out due to lack of finances. The man could not make any money from this investment, so he wanted to sell it quickly.

I visited the school and saw the facilities. They were good. While in Vipingo, I learned that the local residents were so poor they could not afford to feed their children, let alone pay for school fees.

I decided to buy the school and invite all the poor children to learn for free. We recruited teachers and posted them there. I realized that even though we were offering free education, most children were unable to attend because they lacked food. So we started a feeding program within the school in order to make it possible for more children to be educated. The feeding program ensured that the children would remain in school.

In one of my outreach trips in Mombasa I found a street boy who was born out of wedlock to a prostitute. He was addicted to drugs and suffered at the hands of tourists who took advantage of him with homosexual activity. I gave him the opportunity to join MCF Vipingo. When he finished grade 8 I transferred him to MCF Ndalani, where he finished high school. He then went on to university. These visible accomplishments are amazing in themselves. Yet the inner healing of forgiving his abusers is more remarkable. And when I think about him I am so humbled by how God transforms a heart of unbearable sorrow to genuine love.

Besides in Kitale and Kilifi, MCF also focused on touching lives in Turkana County. This is one of the largest and poorest counties in Kenya. It is located in an arid part of Kenya prone to drought and famine. For numerous reasons, it is considered one of the most underdeveloped places in Kenya. The rainfall pattern in Turkana is unpredictable. At times it receives no rain in a whole year. As a result, the residents of Turkana are faced with a persistent threat of starvation.

The misery of a poor climate is compounded by continuous cases of insecurity, high levels of poverty, illiteracy, and a lack of basic infrastructure such as roads, hospitals, schools and clean water. In other words, Turkana is synonymous with hardships and suffering.

Turkana is the second largest county in Kenya. It covers 68,680 square kilometres. It is however the least populated area in Kenya. It borders Marsabit to the east, Samburu to the southeast and Baringo and West Pokot to the southwest. It also borders South Sudan to the north, Uganda to the west and Ethiopia to the northeast. The area is truly a hardship zone. It is mainly inhabited by the Turakana and Elmolo communities, which have been plagued by years of poverty, conflict and extreme marginalization.

While travelling along the Lodwar-Kitale road, we often encountered emaciated young children and adults begging for food and water by the roadside. The local residents felt so detached from their country that they commonly quipped that they were coming from Turkana and going to Kenya. However, following the discovery of oil in the region, there is optimism that life in Turkana will change for the better.

Due to the high value placed on livestock, the Turkana have always been at loggerheads with their neighbours, mainly Pokot, Samburu, Karamojong of Uganda, Toposa from South Sudan and Merille of Ethiopia. The tensions have made the region quite insecure.

Cases of travellers being attacked and killed by armed bandits along the Lodwar Kapenguria road are common. And in 2015, the Kapedo and Nadome areas of Turkana South were in the news for all the wrong reasons. It was reported in the Kenyan media that close to 100 people had died after two nights of attacks and retaliations between pastoralist communities in Turkana and Baringo counties.

In order to contribute to alleviating human suffering, we opened a branch in Lodwar that provides free food, education, clothing and clean drinking water to needy and vulnerable children. By August 2015, over 600 children from the villages of Napetet and Loparaparai in Lodwar, who were mostly malnourished and sickly, were being taken care of. Most of the beneficiaries came from a nearby camp for internally displaced persons.

The project also targets street children for psychosocial support, rehabilitation and education. This is aimed at reducing the high number of homeless children who loiter in the streets of Lodwar town in search of food. This intervention has restored hope in the lives of the most vulnerable children. It is encouraging to note that all the children who have been integrated in the school program are passionately eager to continue with their education.

At MCF, we consider education the greatest component in the rehabilitation process. As such, we are working closely with our partners to ensure proper construction of classrooms and the supply of proper learning and teaching materials. Our goal is to see children from Turkana pass their exams and pursue their career dreams.

For those who are unable to pursue higher education, we intend to build a vocational school to equip them with skills like tailoring, masonry and hairdressing that will enable them to engage in meaningful self-employment.

Besides offering material assistance to alleviate human suffering, MCF is currently working with the community and local leaders in Turkana to promote awareness of child rights and child protection, especially equal opportunities for boy-child and girl-child education, and HIV/AIDS, as well as social and gender issues. With God, everything is possible. We believe that through His mighty power, we can work together and transform the lives of the suffering children in Turkana.

I have compassion for people who have continually suffered due to the weather and climate. They are poverty-stricken. I thought of taking the gospel to them in a more dynamic way by also providing food and water. I saw the need of the people. They needed Christ. They needed education. And they needed food and water. These are my people. And I cannot be in peace unless I operate in other parts of the country.

In 2009, there was great hunger in Turkana. I told my staff to take 200 bags of maize, cooking oil, beans and other dry foods and distribute them to the hungry families in Turkana. I also flew there from Nairobi to take part in the food donation exercise.

The truck would take 48 hours to reach Lodwar from Ndalani, while my flight would take 40 minutes. I arrived a day before the truck.

While in Lodwar, I decided to visit the villages and interact with the local residents as I waited for the food to arrive. I was interested to see how they were coping with life and wanted to give them a word of encouragement. Furthermore, I had watched and read a lot about Turkana in the media, but I now wanted to experience the reality of the reported conditions.

We drove south to a place called Lokorio. Here I came face-to-face with human suffering. It had not rained for seven years in this far-flung area. The people knew nothing about government. They had been left to themselves. They only lamented about a combination of natural and man-made catastrophes. They strongly accused the government of abandoning them.

The residents explained about the numerous problems they were facing. Some of them owned cows, but they had sent the young men to graze them in a faraway land where they would get some pasture and water. They also faced frequent cattle raids.

In one of the houses, I found a very old and sickly woman. Her health had deteriorated due to constant sickness and hunger and old age. I sat down on a traditional stool, *akicholong*, next to a mat where she slept on the floor. I was accompanied by my son Isaac and a Turkana friend from Lodwar who translated our conversation with local residents.

I introduced myself as an evangelist and told her that God does not forsake His people despite the suffering they go through. I told her that God knew what she was going through and He would manifest Himself at His own appointed time. She looked at us with indifference and cursed. She said many people had visited Lokori while mentioning the name of God but left her in hopelessness. She was not interested in hearing anything about God.

I managed to convince her, and she allowed me to pray for her healing. Her body was mere skin and bones. A skeleton, really. As I shared the Word and power of God, she sat down and listened. I prayed along with many people who were praying outside her hut, including my son Isaac. I told her that God would bring rain and that food would come.

She did not want to believe it. Not at first. So I continued to encourage her. I know when God has spoken to me. There is no doubt. None. And when God speaks, we must have faith.

We plant a seed of doubt when we don't believe that God will provide. This woman had a huge responsibility. She had 20 grandchildren, and she could not feed them. In the prayer, I beseeched God to reveal His powers and mercies to the people of Lokori. I asked the Almighty to touch their lives in His own unique way. After the prayer, we gave her some food that we had carried in the car and promised to donate more when the MCF truck arrived in Turkana. I also tasked my friend in Lodwar to ensure that she was treated well.

The day after we left Lokori village, it rained heavily for the first time in seven years. That rain was christened *mvua ya Mulli* (Mulli's rain) by the local residents. They had been crying about rain, but I kept telling them that "God will do something soon." This sickly lady even was healed and started walking around the villages. I later received a message that she had sent people to tell me, that my God is a true God.

She died in 2015. As she was nearing her passing she called her family and pastor together. She asked the pastor to pass a message to me. She said to him, "When Mulli came and he promised about the power of God, the food supply and the rain came. I had never ever seen something like that. I have trusted in God. I have prayed that God will bless Charles Mulli in his work. He is a true prophet. A true servant." And right after that she died.

When I received her message I felt God's confirmation that He does things that no man can do. It gave me more hope and confidence in the ministry of the Lord God to be able to tell it to all the people without any fear or any doubt.

These stories demonstrate how God has enabled us to bring the message of the Good News of Jesus to thousands of people. The MCF outreach began with God's prompting me to share the gospel to a handful of local street children. It has expanded to reach the needs of children across Kenya, Tanzania and Uganda. The children have not only heard the gospel; they have also received the Good News of Jesus as we have provided for their physical and spiritual needs.

Chapter Nine
FIGHTING FOR JUSTICE

Isaiah 1:17 instructs us what it means to obey God: "Learn to do right; seek justice. Defend the oppressed. Take up the cause of the fatherless; plead the case of the widow." Seeking justice for oppressed children is a calling I am convicted to pursue. In addition to the rehabilitation of children, MCF has strongly campaigned for the rights of children.

The first way that MCF has fought for the rights of children is a sustained effort to promote community participation in addressing the root causes of many problems affecting the vulnerable children and destitute families. This has been accomplished through community education and empowerment activities at local and national levels. These activities are focused on awareness of child rights, community health and community empowerment to promote community care of vulnerable children and destitute families along with environmental conservation and development.

We are keen on child rights because we understand the needs of the child. Government and police officials may state that street or homeless children are rounded up for the purposes of identifying and reuniting them with their families or placing them in appropriate institutions for their care. But the manner in which the children are treated, both by police and within institutions, contradicts such intentions, as these children are arrested and dealt with like criminals.

In an effort to help people understand the rights of children we began the Justice for Children program. This program is a prevention strategy that focuses on initiating and implementing projects that eventually reduce the vulnerability of children at a community level. We teach the community about children's rights. Through education and knowledge, the community is mobilized to become agents for change in helping the children. The Bible says, "My people are destroyed from lack of knowledge" (Hosea 4:6). So our aim is to equip the community so that they can take preventative measures.

We accomplish this by organizing a *baraza*, which is a meeting organized by area chiefs. In these meetings we talk about community development, agriculture practices and actions that can be taken. The specific activities include child rights education.

Children are often abused. They are left to suffer. But through the program people are made aware of the children's rights.

These include the need to care for children regardless of their circumstances by giving them food, shelter, education, medical care and love. A child has the right not to be beaten, not to be abused, not to be shouted at and not to be mistreated in any way.

A child also has the right to freedom of speech and expression. The development of children is in part based on whether they believe someone is willing to allow them to share their heart and their mind. There is much compassion when we give a child our full and undivided attention.

Of the many challenges facing Kenya, one is the abuse of the rights of widows and their children to an inheritance. This is a common phenomenon. Lack of information and ignorance of the law, particularly on inheritance in the rural countryside, has created a major disadvantage for widows and orphans. Typically the sons will receive the inheritance but the daughters are left out. MCF has intervened by meeting with the government as well as Kenyan non-government agencies to explain the problem and to encourage them to change the practise of inheritance.

Yet one of the biggest challenges Kenya faces today is providing care and support for two groups of children: orphaned and vulnerable children and children in conflict with the law. Not all orphaned and vulnerable children commit crimes, so it is important to distinguish between the two groups. Yet both need to access justice as the growing numbers overwhelm available resources.

HIV/AIDS, fuelled by high poverty levels, has resulted in the deaths of many parents. It is one of the main contributors to the dramatic rise in orphaned and vulnerable children as well as street children. Deteriorating circumstances at home and in the community expose children to exploitation and abuse. Escalating crime and social disorganization are also contributing factors to the increasing numbers of orphaned and vulnerable children within the rural communities, in urban centres and in juvenile remand homes.

The association between orphaned and vulnerable children, street children and crime has increased in recent years. Despite a consistent lack of evidence of being involved or planning to be involved in criminal activities, children are still taken off the streets and put into police cells and end up in juvenile remand homes. Most of the time, these children are arrested for being homeless, on the grounds of vagrancy or loitering or because they are in need of care and protection. Very few are arrested for committing serious crimes. The most common crimes include involvement in illegal activities such as drug trafficking, unlicensed selling or petty theft.

But the harsh physical reality of these children is only part of their incredible suffering. There is also a high degree of psychosocial trauma suffered by orphaned and vulnerable children when they lose their parents. They face significant responsibilities, particularly the need to fend for younger siblings. They are left caring for younger children even when they themselves are not in a position to help. For example, when the girls are young they are raped. And when a girl is raped she receives nothing in return. In prostitution, another form of violence against women, the prostitute gets money that she can use to survive. Her mind is trapped in a vicious cycle where she is unable to do anything but remain in bondage to sell herself for money. The raped victim has nothing. No one to care for her. And so these girls are in a state of total despair.

Part of the problem is that this crime is so common. But just because rape and prostitution happen so often does not lessen the unbearable torment that each and every girl goes through.

A combination of factors leads to girls' downfall. There is a lack of food. There is the ongoing fear of violence because they know they will be beaten if they complain. They are constantly threatened. They are forced into sex. All of this builds a psychological illness—they become sick in their minds. They cannot bear anything anymore.

They are taken over.

The boys do not have any better. They are sodomized. Beaten. Left without anything to eat. No shelter. No love. In their minds they are depressed and unwanted.

If they report to the police, they are not heard. They are left in a dark world. Left in the streets to try to survive. No rule of law. They are traumatized. Stigmatized. Depressed.

And the way they come out of the depression is by love. Love is everything. It breaks everything. Breaks walls of hatred. It brings a young person closer to you. They share their needs. They move from their world of trauma into a world of joy.

And this love is not by mouth but by action. Love is taking action to do something for them. They see that your promise is bound in your action. You are caring for them as if they are your own.

Though there is no comprehensive data on child abuse cases in Yatta District because of a lack of reporting, orphans are the major victims of child abuse. Child abuse cases are also on the rise, with data from the Yatta District Children's Office and MCF recording different forms of the vice. These include rape, early marriages of young girls, physical punishment in schools, neglect, assault, and child trafficking for child labour and child prostitution.

An initial mapping survey carried out by MCF in local schools in 2011 revealed limited or lack of child rights groups and a corresponding minimum participation of children in issues of school governance and behaviour management. This has compounded child protection problems and their access to justice when necessary. Effective reporting and management of child abuse cases remains lacking in the local community mainly due to police phobia, lack of knowledge of post defilement care by members of the community and police, stigma, cultural barriers and a general lack of information.

Another major challenge MCF faces is the integration of children from juvenile remand homes into MCF's programs for holistic care and rehabilitation. The way of life inside the remand homes is terrible. The children live in fear. It's like working in the middle of traffic on a highway.

Children rescued by MCF from remand homes provide unfavourable feedback on their treatment in detention by both staff and the justice system through the delayed determination of their cases. This has had a negative impact in their integration in a normal rehabilitation environment. Delayed processing by magistrate courts of committal documents of children rescued by MCF has also been a challenge in facilitating the timely rescue of children.

But when they come from remand to MCF, they feel so happy. They have safety. Love. Freedom of expression. They are given food, clothing and a bed. They start afresh. It is a great joy for me to see that they were in a hopeless state but now they have a future. I love to see them go from the worst state of humanity to becoming the people who will be the transformers in the future.

Human rights awareness is an important step in obtaining a dignified livelihood for both children and adults. Children rights are human rights, therefore MCF's focus on the promotion of access to justice for children is aimed at holding duty bearers to account for their obligations, empowering children to demand their rightful entitlements, promoting equity and challenging discrimination. There is a need to challenge mindsets that exclude children and women from decision-making in community matters like property rights. MCF's strategy to facilitate the promotion of best practices in child protection in society through community education will decrease levels of vulnerability for all children, with special benefits to the orphaned, the homeless and all other categories of destitute children.

In 2014, MCF facilitated the successful training of 40 police officers and stakeholders in the application of the Sexual Offences Act (SOA) in child protection to ensure that affected children access justice through an effective court process. Many issues emerged that informed the MCF 2015 work plan to consolidate gains in the training.

Police came for two days' training on the SOA and how people who commit these acts should be dealt with. When a woman or child reports abuse, police should not hesitate to protect and care for the victim. Then they need to take action. They need to record a narrative of what happened. And then they need to take the perpetrators to a court of law.

I applied to the government to have them provide a small room in the police station that could be segregated for only women to report in.

I wanted this to be a separate room because women can feel ashamed to talk to a male police officer. I have been given authority by the government of Kenya to start this up. We will train policewomen to stand in the gap for the victims. We had a group at MCF who has been trained in this. This is unique in Kenya.

When I see a problem, I get attached to that problem. The problem affects children and women and men, and it impacts me. The problems other people have impact me. I am on the side of the person who has been abused. When I see someone with a problem, I see it as being my problem, just like the post-election violence in Eldoret. It was not their problem. It was my problem. I flew out there. This reaction is automatically generated in me. I see the problem and I ask, how can I help?

As an organization, we have scaled up to provide legal guardianship for vulnerable children through the court committal processing. Forty-five percent of children under our full-time care are committed through the courts. MCF successfully influenced the inclusion of children's matters as a core component in the community policing strategy in Yatta sub-county. MCF was co-opted to the membership of the Community Policing Committee. Most importantly, we closely work with juvenile remand homes—mainly Thika and Machakos—for purposes of improving care services and referrals of children for further rehabilitation.

We also strengthened networks with courts in Yatta sub-county during the annual Judicial Marches Week to share experiences for efficient responses to cases involving children. We are trying to become a voice for the voiceless, trying to encourage a faster response to children's cases. We make their suffering known, and the judiciary takes note. The children need to be heard.

It was against this background that a team of 16 judiciary staff members from Yatta District Kithimani law courts, led by the principal magistrate and resident magistrate, identified MCF as a stakeholder to visit during the 2014 national Judicial Marches Week in Kenya in line with the judiciary corporate social responsibility.

The government prefers to give the children to MCF than to put them in juvenile homes—even those children who have committed manslaughter. That may seem outrageous. Yet the most powerful weapon that God has given me in the journey of faith is the power of prayer. With this power of prayer, the negative impact of the social problems that the children have witnessed or committed is removed. I see that the attacks from the enemy—the devil—enter these families. They are demon possessed.

In all of this I cling to Philippians 1:9–10: "This is my prayer: that your love may abound more and more in knowledge and depth of insight, so that you may be able to discern with is best and may be pure and blameless for the day of Christ." It is not ability. It is not about having a doctorate. When trouble is on that high level of attack, you apply the prayers. God hears the prayers of the righteous. He hears us when we intercede for those accosted by evil spirits. We bind those spirits. We bind the spirit of discord. We bind it in the name of Jesus Christ, the name above all names. This is the weapon that we use to denounce the power of the evil spirits in the mighty name of Jesus Christ. Some people may think it cannot work, but it can work. As it says in Philippians 4:13, "I can do all this through him who gives me strength."

Principal Magistrate Hon. Karani Gitonga and Resident Magistrate Hon. Martha Opanga enlightened MCF staff and children on the aims of the Judicial Marches Week. Hon. Karani said that in line with the rallying call by Chief Justice of Kenya Dr. Willy Mutunga, the judiciary staff wants to lead the way in living up to the expectations of the Constitution to be accountable to the public by providing information and responding to questions.

The team also listened to testimonies as well as performances by MCF children. Hon. Karani recognized MCF as an important partner that was complementing the work of the judiciary by facilitating access to justice for vulnerable children.

Meanwhile, I made a special request to the judiciary to consider the option of special mobile courts sitting in MCF in the future to facilitate the processing of court committal orders for rescued orphaned and vulnerable children currently under MCF care. The principal magistrate confirmed that the request will definitely be followed up, as the judiciary seeks to increase access to justice for all, including the most vulnerable in society.

I assured the judiciary officers that MCF will continue to work closely with the courts in different parts of Kenya by rescuing children in need of temporary custody or long-term care as referred to us by the magistrates.

The team presented us with a statement from Chief Justice of Kenya Hon. Dr. Willy Mutunga, which read,

> Today is a day of great joy for Kenya and the judiciary. It is a moment for us who are privileged to serve in the judiciary to open up to the public; explain to them how we work; and get feedback from the people on how to improve our services...The Constitution of Kenya has created a new country. It bids the judiciary, and the Kenyan society as a whole, to transform. We have embarked on an elaborate programme to transform the judiciary by making it people-centred and service-oriented. Indeed, this is the first pillar of the Judiciary Transformation Framework, launched a little over two months ago. The new judiciary is becoming more open, accessible, modern, efficient and effective.
>
> We are launching the Judicial Marches Week, an event to be held once every year around the country, as part of our transformation program. Through the Judicial Marches Week, we seek not only to make the Judiciary more accessible to the public, but also to remind ourselves of the constitutional edict that judicial authority comes from the people.
>
> We are establishing Court Users Committees at the national, county and court station level, which give all the actors in the justice chain—from the prosecutions directorate, the attorney general, the police to the prisons to civil society organizations—a forum to work together to resolve issues that prevent them from delivering on their mandates.
>
> Our goal is not to simply have us doing what we can do on our own, but to get other stakeholders involved. We want to make others aware. If you are by yourself in a big country like Kenya, it is hard to make progress. But if you mobilize others and join together, the progress is much better. We desire to create a relationship with the public, nurtured by dialogue that seeks to find solutions to the challenges Kenya faces as a society. The Court Users Committees continue to present a great platform for the judiciary to learn about the changing needs of the society and to adjust to them accordingly.

The main aim in undertaking the Judicial Marches by the Kenyan courts was to demonstrate the radical shift required by the Constitution in recognizing that the judicial authority comes from the people.

The judiciary also signalled to the Kenyan people that the authority of the courts was not to be found in mysticism but rather in the quality of their decisions. It also sought to encourage the public to use alternative dispute resolution mechanisms, including traditional ones, as long as they do not offend the Constitution. It further sensitized the public on the shared responsibility for the administration and delivery of justice with other partners, such as the police, the directorate of prosecutions and the prison service.

God has enabled MCF to bring about increased justice for children in Africa. We continue to fight for the rights of children and to represent their cause. We believe that defending the cause of the oppressed is part of our mission to bring the Good News to the people of Africa. As we continue to work with the government and the legal system, I hold to the call of Isaiah 58:6–11:

> "Is not this the kind of fasting I have chosen:
> to loose the chains of injustice
> and untie the cords of the yoke,
> to set the oppressed free
> and break every yoke?
> Is it not to share your food with the hungry
> and to provide the poor wanderer with shelter—
> when you see the naked, to clothe them,
> and not to turn away from your own flesh and blood?
> Then your light will break forth like the dawn,
> and your healing will quickly appear;
> then your righteousness will go before you,
> and the glory of the LORD will be your rear guard.
> Then you will call, and the LORD will answer;
> you will cry for help, and he will say: Here am I.
> If you do away with the yoke of oppression,
> with the pointing finger and malicious talk,
> and if you spend yourselves in behalf of the hungry
> and satisfy the needs of the oppressed,
> then your light will rise in the darkness,
> and your night will become like the noonday.
> The LORD will guide you always;
> he will satisfy your needs in a sun-scorched land
> and will strengthen your frame.
> You will be like a well-watered garden,
> like a spring of water whose waters never fail."

Chapter Ten
RESPONDING TO VIOLENCE
MCF's Intervention in the Post-Election Violence

Sharing the Good News of Jesus has called us to respond to many crises in Kenya. One of the most challenging times for MCF was during the 2007-2008 post-election violence.

During this time, Kenyans rose against each other in a very unprecedented fashion. Love disappeared into thin air as residents armed themselves with machetes and arrows. They killed one another, burned houses and looted property. The senseless tribal killings, destruction of property and displacement of thousands of people based on ethnic profiling was horrifying. Over 1,300 people were killed, and close to 600,000 others were displaced.

We had witnessed clashes in the past years, especially in 1992 and 1997 in Molo, Burnt Forest, Mount Elgon and other places, but this particular violent uprising was too much to bear. Supporters of President Mwai Kibaki clashed with those of Raila Odinga, the fierce contestants in the December 2007 disputed presidential elections. There were claims that elections had been rigged in favour of the incumbent Mwai Kibaki.

We saw images of armed youths burning houses and destroying property that belonged to their perceived political opponents. These events took place mainly in Eldoret, Nakuru, Kericho, Kisumu, Naivasha, Nairobi and parts of Mombasa. Youths blocked roads, burned cars and killed people who did not belong to their tribes. Criminals took advantage of the lack of law and order to loot property.

The country literally came to a standstill. The hearts of love, the voices of reason, the faces of kindness and the hands of generosity were thrown away as neighbours turned against each other. Youths lit bonfires, ejected passengers from vehicles and murdered them, depending on whether they were from the "right" tribe or not. Police used live ammunition to disperse protesters who began to overwhelm them. It was chaos everywhere.

Those who escaped death ran to seek refuge in places they thought would be safe, including churches, police stations, schools and mosques. I saw and felt the emptiness that comes with displacement. People—adults as much as children—looked so vulnerable. They had run away and were happy not to have been killed but arrived at the Eldoret Showground camp for internally displaced persons with virtually nothing. They could not manage to take care of themselves.

I was in Ndalani when I watched the gory scenes on TV. The conflict was covered all over the globe. The international media showed images of Kenyans killing each other. They told the story as they saw it. Global eyes focused on Kenya. The media declared Kenya to be a "burning nation." Women and children bore the heaviest brunt of the violence as they were helplessly sheltered wherever they could be. One particularly traumatizing event was when dozens of people were burned alive in a church in Eldoret, where they had gone to seek refuge.

Our screens were full of tears and anguish. This was arguably the worst humanitarian crisis ever witnessed in Kenya. And it happened at a time when our country was viewed as a fortress of economic and political stability in a volatile region.

I could see many children staring blankly into an uncertain future, having lost their parents in the clashes. Women cried as they recounted how they witnessed their husbands and sons being killed in cold blood. Trauma and hopelessness were written all over their faces. The problem was big and complex, and I didn't know where to begin in terms of offering assistance to the victims. But deep within my heart I knew that our Supreme God has an answer to everything. He would open a road where there seemed to be no way.

I received numerous telephone calls and emails from friends around the world who were shocked by the killings. I too asked endless questions. How can people turn against each other in such a cruel manner? Why would neighbours who lived together for many years rise up against each other on the basis of tribal and political affiliations?

I then uttered a prayer: "Oh, dear Lord, save our country and our people from destruction. Whatever is happening around us is not what

You desire for humanity. Rid our country of satanic spirits, and let Your Holy Spirit dwell in us. Teach us to forever love one another, to be patient and ready to forgive. Touch us with Your hand of love so that we appreciate one another, and restore the sanctity of human life. Amen." I further asked God to give me strength and courage so that I could do something, however small, to touch the hurting souls—especially those of children—who had been adversely affected by the clashes.

As the days continued we kept receiving reports of more and more people moving to internal displacement camps in Eldoret, Nakuru, Naivasha, Kisumu and other areas. The animosity between warring factions seemed unending as the peace mediation process dragged on in Nairobi. Riots in Nairobi continued as Orange Democratic Movement supporters called for the installation of Raila Odinga as president.

A team comprised of some of Africa's eminent persons, led by former United Nations Secretary General Kofi Annan, had landed in Nairobi with the intent to unite the Kibaki and Raila teams. Talk of power-sharing was on the table.

I flew to Eldoret in early January to assess the situation. From the plane I saw torched houses in the Molo, Timboroa and Burnt Forest areas. Even before touching the ground, I gathered that the situation ahead of me was awful and full of suffering. After landing in Eldoret, I saw many people camping at the airport, waiting to be airlifted to safety. This was the tip of the iceberg of what lay ahead. Those who could afford an air ticket were flying away to safety.

But what about the poor? I asked myself.

During my taxi ride to Eldoret town we passed through various roadblocks mounted by armed youths. The roadblocks were made of huge stones, logs of woods and burning tires. At the Kapseret market we came across a huge barrier with hundreds of youths who were set on identifying travellers to know whether they belonged to their tribe or the enemies' tribe. They were chanting all manner of songs, both political and cultural. The overriding theme was castigating the political (or tribal) enemy. Everyone seemed ready for war, to kill or be killed. It was a very chilling experience. You could die or survive in the hands of these youths, depending on the tribe you belonged to. I came to learn that several people who belonged to an enemy tribe had been hacked to death at the very spot we drove through.

Being from Ukambani, I was considered to belong to an enemy tribe. They came to our car brandishing machetes while others were carrying wooden throwing clubs called *rungus*, metal bars, stones and all manner of weapons. They yelled war cries while brushing their machetes against the tarmac. It produced an eerie sound. I looked at their blood-hungry faces and saw the devil at work. The desire of armed youths to kill was beyond understanding. I silently asked God not to desert His people, and I prayed that He would guard our country from disintegration.

The man who drove me was popular with these youths. He just waved at them, and they opened the barrier for us to proceed. At some point I was scared that the blood-hungry youths would attack us, but he assured me that I was safe with him. He even told me that he had helped to sneak out several people who would have otherwise surely been killed on the spot if they had gone alone.

I counted about five barriers between the airport and the Eldoret showground where the camp for international displaced persons had been established. I looked outside the window and saw burned houses and other destroyed properties along the way. All signs pointed to large-scale violence and destruction. The air around Eldoret was full of tension. People were not moving freely. Businesses had been destroyed, and I was not sure what the next minute would bring. Many people preferred to stay indoors or go as far away from Eldoret as possible. I was now able to internalize what I had watched earlier on TV. Tension. Violence. Destruction. Death.

When I entered the showground, I came face-to-face with human suffering. Tears. Pain. Suffering. Anguish. Emptiness. Over 10,000 people had sought refuge there. The amenities were hardly enough to sustain even 10 percent of this number. The conditions were deplorable. There was no food, medical care or even shelter for the victims. Most of the victims were in shock. They were mourning the loss of loved ones and the loss of property. I met a grieving woman whose husband had been killed and their house torched. The situation was tragic.

At that point, I felt that MCF had to move with speed. We needed to set up camp in Eldoret and contribute to alleviating the suffering of the post-election violence victims, particularly children and women. I called my people back in Ndalani and Yatta and told them to be ready to move to Eldoret as soon as possible to offer humanitarian assistance.

Most of these victims had all their property looted, their houses burned down and their sources of livelihood destroyed, and they had to move to the camp for safety without salvaging their property. Many people in the region—people like you and me, sons, daughters, mothers, fathers, relatives—were either killed or maimed, while young girls and women were sexually violated. These people needed very special attention, especially psychosocial support, as they joined the overcrowded camps.

Throughout history, humankind has reacted to many different problems such as conflict, war, and excessive rain. God speaks to people in different ways. Perhaps God also wanted to talk to Kenyans through this violence. Kenyans felt they were prospering and growing more powerful. There was a prideful attitude. Things had become like at the Tower of Babel. They forgot about God. This does not put the blame at all on those who were killed or injured. Yet after the fighting people became closer to one another. God wanted the Kenyan people to love one another—to think positively about their own welfare and economic development. He wanted them to trust in Him more.

When we started our work in Eldoret to help victims of the violence, we had a mere $3,000 in the bank. And even that money was for the children in Yatta and Ndalani. But we were going out to Eldoret to help thousands of refugees. It felt like the five loaves and two fish or David and his stones against Goliath.

We used all the $3,000 to buy food and medicine. I prayed, "God this is the moment that we need You more than ever before. You know me. I am Your servant. I pray that You will provide enough for these people."

I wrote to friends that we were on the battlefield. "Kenya is burning. People are in desperate need. Please remember us in prayer." I did not ask to receive any money. Yet within a week I received $100,000. And people continued to send money. This helped us tremendously in carrying out our mission to help people.

I flew back to Nairobi the same evening and coordinated a team that left for Eldoret a week later to offer humanitarian assistance to the post-election victims. I instructed them to go to the ground with the motto of saving lives, not only of children but of every human being. In that brief moment in Eldoret, I had witnessed large-scale human suffering.

At the start of the emergency intervention project we were over-stretched in terms of resources, but with time, friends and donors came on board, and the support we received enabled us to feed over 11,000 people daily. We cooked breakfast, lunch and supper for this massive population every day.

The very thought of helping so many people seemed impossible. Even some partners doubted our capacity. But God again parted the Red Sea to make it possible for us to carry out His will. He enabled us to coordinate and work together with other organizations to bring the maximum benefit to people. Through His grace we were able to feed a huge population. We knew that many victims were hurting. They had lost a lot in life, and nothing seemed to matter anymore. We did our best to make them feel appreciated, even as the whole world seemed to be against them.

In close collaboration with the Kenya Red Cross, MCF facilitated emergency intervention targeting 11,000 people at the Eldoret show-ground camp for internally displaced persons.

We offered food supplements to expectant and nursing mothers and supported newborn babies at the camp with clothing and other basics provisions. We provided medical care for manageable ailments and paid the bills of those who were referred to major hospitals for further attention.

In the process of implementing the emergency intervention activities, we identified a total of 65 most needy and vulnerable children and transferred them to the Ndalani and Yatta centres. These children had lost both parents and even their extended family and had nowhere to return to. These rescued children were able to access all the basic needs of food, medical care, education, professional guidance and counselling, protection, spiritual nourishment and, above all, parental love.

Meanwhile, we started a makeshift school within the camp and ensured that all school-aged children were enrolled in studies. It was tough for most of them to adapt to and cope in this open-air school, but with time everything went smoothly. Within the camp, we had trained teachers who had been displaced from their homes. I decided to hire them to teach in this school. Displaced teachers taught displaced students. We paid them salaries, and they were able to begin to rebuild their good lives once again. I used to meet with them in the evenings, and I encouraged them not to look at the past but to focus on rebuilding their future.

As we interacted, I told them the story of a man in the Bible called Job. He was from Uz. He was a man who feared God and did not commit evil deeds. He was the richest man at that time. Satan believed that

Job was only righteous because the Lord had given him a lot of wealth and had protected his family. But after a while Job lost virtually everything that he had in life.

> One day when Job's sons and daughters were feasting and drinking wine at the oldest brother's house, a messenger came to Job and said, "The oxen were plowing and the donkeys were grazing nearby, and the Sabeans attacked and made off with them. They put the servants to the sword, and I am the only one who has escaped to tell you!"
>
> While he was still speaking, another messenger came and said, "The fire of God fell from the heavens and burned up the sheep and the servants, and I am the only one who has escaped to tell you!"
>
> While he was still speaking, another messenger came and said, "The Chaldeans formed three raiding parties and swept down on your camels and made off with them. They put the servants to the sword, and I am the only one who has escaped to tell you!"
>
> While he was still speaking, yet another messenger came and said, "Your sons and daughters were feasting and drinking wine at the oldest brother's house, when suddenly a mighty wind swept in from the desert and struck the four corners of the house. It collapsed on them and they are dead, and I am the only one who has escaped to tell you!"
>
> At this, Job got up and tore his robe and shaved his head. Then he fell to the ground in worship and said: "...The LORD gave and the LORD has taken away; may the name of the LORD be praised." (Job 1:10–21)

I told the teachers that we are all human beings under the mercy of God. I encouraged them to keep believing in God whether they had plenty or whether they had nothing at all, as was the case in the Eldoret camp.

While in Eldoret, I visited the burned church in Kiambaa. This incident spoke volumes about the tragic culmination of the post-election violence. It showed how low we had sunk as a nation. It revealed how the devil had consumed our country. Both local and international media had covered the tragedy extensively, so I chose to visit and gain first-hand knowledge of the situation.

When the violence started, those who were escaping considered the church one of the safest places. Most of them were women and children from a nearby estate. They thought no one would dare attack a church. However, the Kiambaa church massacre on January 1, 2008, defied this belief. The fact that churches are universally considered the most sacred places of refuge in times of conflict did not spare this particular church. The fact that there were mainly women and children hiding inside the church did not deter the attackers. According to reports that we received in Eldoret, the raiders followed the victims into the church and set it ablaze with gasoline. Those who tried to escape the burning fire were attacked with machetes or arrows. A total of 35 women and children were burned alive.

Thousands of other displaced persons sought refuge at the Catholic church in Eldoret town. They filled the church compound until there was no space for others to come in.

When we visited the Kiambaa church, a ghostly silence shrouded the environment. We only saw the rubble of collapsed mud walls and the remains of wooden poles, a testimony to the fierce fire that set it ablaze. We also saw personal items like shoes and clothes.

The sight of the charred remains of a child's clothes moved me to tears. I grabbed the particular clothes from the debris and examined them closely, and it hit me that the owner must have perished in the inferno. I became overwhelmed with sad emotions. I could not imagine the levels of cruelty that could lead someone to burn a church with children inside. Whatever the degree of provocation, nothing could justify the burning of people in a church. Accompanied by my son Isaac and a number of MCF staff, I held intercessory prayers at this venue of disaster and asked God not to allow such demonic events to occur on our land again.

That day we also visited a number of families who had been affected by the clashes but were not in the camp for displaced persons. We had information about people who had lost virtually everything and were lucky to have been taken in by relatives or friends. There were many people like this, though the details of their struggles were not captured well.

We prayed with them, gave them food and encouraged them to trust in the Lord always. Many of them were hurting. Their faces and even their speech told it all. Still, I told them that God was aware of what they were going through and He would console them at an appropriate time. I encouraged them to faithfully wait upon the Lord. We returned to the showground in the evening and continued providing food to the victims of the violence under our care.

I took some time alone in the evening and walked around the tents that were home to the displaced people. I preferred to walk alone, quietly, because it gave me time to meditate on some weighty matters. I met with children who were crying in pain. The faces of their parents denoted total emptiness. These were people who had been evicted from their homes by their neighbours. They counted themselves fortunate to be in the camp because many others were killed. Silently I asked myself, *How cruel can a human heart become? How far can we go in killing each other because of elections, power and wealth? To what extent can tribalism and partisan interests cloud our love for each other? Is there no end to our desire to harm our enemies?* The questions crowded my mind.

I went back to my house in Pioneer Estate and prayed for the suffering children of God. I once again asked God to take control of the whole situation.

As the year progressed, the number of displaced persons at the Eldoret showground started reducing. Many victims were going away, either to live with relatives or to seek other forms of livelihood. They say time is a great healer. After some time, most of them were healed, picked up the pieces, sought employment and left the camps.

After the successful Serena talks (named after the hotel in Nairobi that served as the venue where peace talks were held), we saw the formation of a coalition government—with Mwai Kibaki as president and Raila Odinga as prime minister. This new government embarked on resettling the displaced persons in an initiative dubbed Operation Rudi Nyumbani (meaning "return home"). Some of the refugees were given a compensation fee to enable them to leave the camp and establish a home in the place of their choice. This was done with the hope of them being able to rebuild their lives. In other places, the government was buying land and resettling people there. This saw a drastic reduction in the numbers of displaced persons.

Years later, nothing much remained of the Kiambaa church. The local Kiambaa primary school was later renamed Kipnyikei. But despite the change in name, the sad memories still linger on. The sound of happy children playing in the compound is conspicuously absent.

At the end of 2008, I felt that we had played our part in helping to save lives, and we also wound up our mission in Eldoret. I held a big party for about 40 MCF staff who had stayed in Eldoret for the whole year to help the displaced persons. I told them that they had played a great role in saving lives and their greatest reward was in heaven. We had entered Eldoret silently but left triumphantly.

For those who want to step out in faith but feel they lack the faith to do so, they key is to trust in God and have faith in Him in totality. You surrender whatever the needs are to Him and pray for His will to be done. This is not about pushing God, not about trying to force Him. You simply pray. Again, it is not about wanting something for yourself. No fame. No money. You don't want to gain from the whole thing. Even when you have little, you are there to intercede for them. The anointment of the Lord makes an impact in the work you are doing. God will stir the heart of people to respond and help.

There are those who demand money. People who want to gain. People like heavy-handed preachers. But you don't need to force things. God has His own way to talk to people, to touch people's hearts.

Chapter Eleven
GOD ACCOMPLISHES MORE THAN WE CAN IMAGINE

After the 25-years celebrations, I spent some time mulling over what MCF had achieved for a quarter century. Most of the children I had picked up from the streets when they were younger than five years old were now adults with families. Children who seemed hopeless were now looking ahead to a great future. Despite the challenges we faced in the process of rehabilitating street children and other vulnerable groups, the fact that we had touched and transformed thousands of lives made me feel happy. I realized that through God's providence, MCF has come far, it has reached far, and it still intends to go far.

What has God accomplished through MCF? Our home provides a secure residence and stabilizing family love alongside spiritual nourishment, counselling, guidance and Christian teaching. This also includes maintaining comprehensive feeding and medical care programs to provide for the children's physiological needs as fundamental to their rehabilitation.

On matters regarding education, we provide basic and advanced literacy skills in conformity with the Ministry of Education's system of education or other approved system by the ministry. We work closely with the Ministry of Education to ensure our curriculum is in tandem with other schools across the country. Our children sit for the same KCPE and KCSE examinations with the rest of Kenyans. After high school, those who are accepted at higher institutions of learning are sponsored to proceed on. Through this, we have been able to produce medical doctors, engineers, teachers, media professionals, accountants, managers, ministers of the gospel, agricultural professionals and many others.

Those who do not get the required grades for diploma or degree training are taken to vocational school, where we equip them with skills such as tailoring, cookery, hairdressing, carpentry and masonry. This enables them to use their skills to earn a living. Vocational training equips the beneficiaries with practical skills for resource development and future self-reliance.

Besides education and training, we rehabilitate the children spiritually and morally through character behaviour transformation with the view of reuniting them with their respective families. This enables them to be productive members of society. We do the same for each child whether they have parents or not.

We also seek to create a humble and acceptable culture among the rescued children through guidance and counselling, promotion of sporting activities for effective socialization with the general public, and a steady diet of Christian outreach programs through gospel music, poetry, drama and testimonies.

Through these endeavours and others, MCF institutions provide holistic education for the children. In addition to academics, the schools are actively engaged in cocurricular activities. These activities assist the children in identifying their talents and developing them to their maximum potential through relevant clubs that have been established in the school.

The karate club is one such initiative that has borne tremendous fruits. These boys and girls have conquered the East African region in karate. We were once champions for seven years in a row. When it comes to national competitions, the majority of the Kenyan team is usually comprised of MCF children. We also have one of the best choir teams. It has performed in various churches and functions across the country and overseas.

With God's help and guidance, MCF has succeeded in implementing our main project activities. The main areas of focus of our activities have included rescue, rehabilitation and reintegration, community education and empowerment projects, promotion of sustainability projects including renewable energy development projects, missions and evangelism. This has resulted in us achieving rehabilitation in the lives of the rescued children and of vulnerable members of the community in various project locations.

❖ ❖ ❖

As our efforts in Kenya grew and solidified, God opened the door for us to minister to children beyond the Kenyan borders.

It began when I was invited by a Swedish friend to address a pastors' conference in Migori, Kenya, organized by the Maranatha Faith Assemblies, which brought together church leaders from the East African region.

After I shared with them about God and my humanitarian work in Kenya, a Tanzanian pastor approached me and talked emotionally about children who were suffering in Tanzanian slums. He painted a picture of children who were staring at an empty future. Having worked for many years with street children, I quickly understood the miserable conditions that he was talking about. He invited me to go down and witness the scenario first-hand so that I could do something about it. He requested that I go and evangelize in the community as well.

As a man with a passion for helping the less fortunate children, I visited Dar es Salaam a month later and was taken to the Mbagala slums, where I came face-to-face with poverty, desperation, alcoholism, drug abuse, prostitution and other vices that are synonymous with low-end areas. This compared very well with what I had witnessed in Nairobi slums such as Kibera, Mukuru and Mathare. We walked with the pastor through Mbagala as I listened to sad tales of suffering children who had lost their parents to HIV/AIDS. The levels of poverty in this place were very high.

On my return from Dar es Salaam I arranged for a number of needy children from the Mbagala slums to be brought to MCF Ndalani. However, because the demand for assistance was high, I opted to start a non-residential rehabilitation centre and a school in this slum to cater to the interests of needy children.

The pastor who introduced me to Tanzania later flew abroad for further studies and left me in the able hands of Pastor Jeremiah Lukiko, whom I duly appointed to be in charge of MCF activities in that country. This hardworking man of God has been instrumental in identifying and helping the vulnerable children in Tanzanian slums.

In November 2007, I flew to Tanzania with my wife, Esther, for a routine visit to greet the MCF children in our Dar es Salaam home that is located in the Mbagala slums, not far from the capital city. The centre was still young, having been started in 2005, and I visited it regularly to fellowship with the children and community members. Most of the amenities were not well established.

I took time, as a father, to encourage those who were serving in the centre, led by Pastor Lukiko, to keep up the good spirit of servanthood. Though some of them were employees on a salary, with the majority of the others working as volunteers, I appreciated that it was not easy to deal with vulnerable children who came with numerous needs. It required a lot of dedication, patience, perseverance and personal sacrifice. This was a centre where we fed and educated the children during the day and then allowed them to go back to their homes in the evening. It had similarities with an ordinary day school. The majority of these children resided in difficult conditions in the slums, having lost their parents to the HIV/AIDS pandemic. Our dedicated team of teachers, pastors and social workers were always at hand to attend to them.

There are very few Muslims in Ndalani. But there are many in Tanzania. In fact, they are the majority. We took the opportunity to minister to the poor in Tanzania. People would come to me to pray for their needs, especially for healing. I saw miracles of people being cured of tuberculosis and malaria. They became better right away. We also saw people freed from demons. Muslims gave their lives to Christ, and many, many other people got saved.

I preached to many crowds inside and outside the church. People expressed how much they loved this ministry. They said, "He is teaching purely about Jesus, not about religion." I make it a point not to lead people to religious beliefs. I only lead people to Christ Jesus. This makes people feel honoured and loved instead of being trapped in a religious system.

That year, we had constructed new classrooms, a church and other basic facilities, so I used the occasion to officially open and dedicate them to God. The event went very well, and the children gave moving testimonies of how MCF had changed their lives for the better. I listened to what they were saying, and I marvelled at how God can change people from nothing to something.

After the event, which was full of speeches, songs, poems and food, the centre coordinator, Pastor Lukiko, took me to the city to introduce me to the Tanzanian cabinet minister in charge of children's affairs. This senior government official had heard a lot about MCF but wanted to hear it officially from those who were running it.

When we reached her office she shook my hand firmly and said, "I have been hearing a lot about Charles Mulli. I'm glad today I have met you personally. You are doing a great job for the poor children of this country." She expressed her satisfaction at the work of MCF, which she termed an organization that was playing a great role in complementing the Tanzania government's efforts to improve the lives of the needy children.

In our discussion, I shared with her the history of MCF, which had by then existed for 18 years. I told her that we started this mission in Eldoret with three children way back in 1989, and 18 years down the line we had helped over 6,000 children. She was listening keenly as I mentioned to her that MCF had five centres in Kenya and two other branches in Dar es Salaam and Kampala. She kept nodding in approval. I also told her my life story and how God used me to give hope to the hopeless.

She finally looked at me with amazement and said, "We need you here, Charles. Tanzania needs people like you, people with a kind heart to help the needy. Our society is full of desperate children, and something must be done about it, urgently. In fact, as the government, we are willing to donate land to you so that you can come and establish children rehabilitation centres in several parts of this country. What do you think about it?"

Of course, I could not give her an instant answer, but I was glad that she was showing a lot of confidence in MCF. I looked at my wife, Esther, and she answered back with a smile. In my response to the minister's question, I invited her to join us in prayer so that together we could ask God to open the way for us. We held hands in her office and dedicated our plans to God in prayer. And as we flew back to Nairobi, I could still hear her ask me, "What do you think about it?"

We exchanged mail towards the end of 2007, and I once again asked her to pray for MCF so that we would get the courage, human capital and resources to expand to many places. I told her that when God is on our side, no weapon formed against us will prevail. Meanwhile, I strongly considered accepting the government's offer to go and construct another centre in Tanzania. I even sought views from my immediate family members and friends on how to approach the expansion issue. Their response and advice was positive. This experience, among other things I had faced in life, showed me that we do not need to keep asking and "pushing" for some things to happen. We do not need a godfather in order to get favours on earth. Personally, I have operated without these "figureheads," and many events in life have moved smoothly. Most of the time the Lord goes ahead of us and touches the hearts of people, and they offer you the kind of support that you need. That's why we are commanded to cast our burdens onto Jesus, because He cares for us.

Meanwhile, as the Tanzania discussions were picking up momentum, Kenya was approaching the December 2007 general elections. I wrote to the good minister and promised to visit Dar es Salaam in early 2008 to discuss further how to establish a home there. However, as fate would have it, the Kenyan elections were met with serious violence. Most of the resources that we would have used to expand into Tanzania were channelled instead to helping the internally displaced persons from the post-election violence in Eldoret.

The Tanzania dream did not die, however. It was just suspended due to a number of commitments back in Kenya. It is my hope that one day I will go back to that country and set up a home similar to Yatta or Ndalani. Personally, I don't discriminate according to religion, colour, tribe or even nationality. I believe that God sent me into this world to help not only the children of Kenya but also those of the whole world.

The pastor who introduced me to Tanzania visited Kenya in November 2014 for our 25th year celebration. He told me, "The number of very needy children keeps growing by the day, but I hope God will enable us to reach as many of them as possible." By 2015, we had about 300 students receiving free education and food daily in this centre.

Zechariah 4:6 says, "This is the word of the LORD to Zerubbabel: 'Not by might nor by power, but by my Spirit,' says the LORD Almighty." When the ministry continued to grow in Tanzania, many challenges continued to mount against us. I asked myself, *How will we reach out to a nation that needs all my commitment?* That was when I came to realize that this will be accomplished not through my power but by the Lord's power. I surrendered the ministry expansion to Tanzania to Him who is able—and the author of our faith.

Truly the impossible is nothing with God.

Chapter Twelve
FINISHING THE RACE

Life is like a marathon and not a sprint. Those who have run long distances understand that the speed they start with does not matter. What matters is how the runners keep going and that they eventually finish the race. Most long-distance runners prefer to run steadily so that they do not tire themselves early, and when they are near the end, they increase their speed and finish triumphantly. For some, winning the race may not be an issue; they simply want to ensure they have finished it. This is the case with us who run the marathon of life. Finishing is the most important thing. This calls for endurance, persistence and consistency.

This was the case with one Tanzanian runner, John Akhwari. He was injured during the marathon race in the 1968 Summer Olympics in Mexico, but he refused to give up. He was a popular marathoner of his day but was the last man to finish the race. He had only covered 19 kilometres (out of 42) when he fell down on the pavement, severely wounding his knee and dislocating his shoulder. He was urged to quit the race and seek treatment, but he refused. Bloodied and bandaged, he continued hobbling on. The stadium was already empty when he finally limped to the finish line over an hour later. When he was asked why he continued in spite of his injury and knowing that he had no hope of winning, Akhwari replied, "My country did not send me 5,000 miles away to start the race; they sent me to finish it."

Yes, finish the race.

I am telling you this story because on March 6, 2015, I lost my father, Daudi Mulli Kaleli, after a long struggle with illness. He had been in and out of the hospital for close to one year. He was 90 years old. This is a man who ran a race in life that was characterized by a slow start but ended up finishing on a high note. Just like the Tanzanian runner, my father was also thrown off-balance in the race of life due to his extreme alcoholism, but he retraced his steps and continued with the race to the end.

When we grew up, *Mzee* (father) Daudi was literally lost in beer. As a result, we, his family members, had difficult lives. He failed to provide for our basic needs and education. He neglected us. By the grace of God, I managed to get a well-paying job and created some sense of stability in our family. But as a born-again Christian, I kept praying for my father's deliverance from the bottle. I always visited him and shared my testimony with him. I told him that I had progressed in life because of accepting God. I spent a lot of time sharing with him the importance of submitting one's life to God. I always prayed for God to deliver him and enable him to see the light.

In one of my routine visits, I went to see him and found him very happy. He was not drunk. He was not sad. He was not deeply immersed in thoughts. His spirits were high. He then told me the good news: "My son, you have been a very instrumental person in my life. I like the way you treat me and the rest of the family. I'm glad that you have made us your burden and that you constantly provide us with food and other basic needs. I offended you in childhood but you forgave me. I like the God you worship and I have decided to give my life to Him too. From today, I'm a Christian."

I clenched my fist and proclaimed, "God is great."

He joined the African Inland Church in Ndalani and was constantly involved in church activities. He hosted church members for a fellowship in his house. I made it a habit of visiting him regularly as we shared various Scriptures from the Bible. Slowly but surely, he started growing strong in faith. God was performing miracles.

After receiving Christ, Mzee Daudi's other leadership skills emerged. Unlike in the past when he had little concern about the plight of the local residents, he now listened to their problems—especially concerning land—and would go all the way to Machakos town to ensure that a particular case has been handled and resolved. As a result, the local residents in Ndalani put a lot of faith in him and elected him as an elder to represent their grievances in matters regarding land, business and other interests. What touched me most was when he called us—all his children—and urged us to stay together and love one another. He told us the importance of unity in a family setup.

He was also appointed as a church elder. His hands were suddenly full, dealing with church and community issues. I always rejoiced whenever I visited and found other people waiting in line for his attention. This to me was a true case of transformation. It was a case of getting back on track to finish the race well. This perfectly explained the popular phrase "The race of life is not measured by the humbleness of your start but by the greatness of your finish."

I was happy that Mzee Daudi died as a man who had accepted Jesus Christ as his personal Saviour. He had gone through a difficult past, which included alcoholism and belief in traditional forces. But he cast all these burdens aside and embraced Christ at a time when it mattered most. His case was a true reflection of the story of the workers in the vineyard (Matthew 20). In this story, the owner of the vineyard pays all his workers the same salary, those who came early in the morning and those who joined as the day was ending. It tells us how God will treat us when we reach heaven. It does not matter when you get saved. What matters is that you are part of the group.

"For the kingdom of heaven is like a landowner who went out early in the morning to hire workers for his vineyard. He agreed to pay them a denarius for the day and sent them into his vineyard. About nine in the morning, he went out and saw others standing in the market place doing nothing. He told them, 'You also go and work in my vineyard, and I will pay you whatever is right.' So they went.

"He went out again about noon and about three in the afternoon and did the same thing. About five in the afternoon he went out and found still others standing around. He asked them, 'Why have you been standing here all day long doing nothing?' 'Because no one has hired us,' they answered. He said to them, 'You also go and work in my vineyard.'

"When evening came, the owner of the vineyard said to his foreman, 'Call the workers and pay them their wages, beginning with the last ones hired and going on to the first.' The workers who were hired about five in the afternoon came and each received a denarius. So when those came who were hired first, they expected to receive more. But each one of them also received a denarius. When they received it, they began to grumble against the landowner. 'These who were hired last worked only one hour,' they said, 'and you have made them equal to us who have borne the burden of the work and the heat of the day.'

"But he answered one of them, "I am not being unfair to you, friend. Didn't you agree to work for a denarius? Take your pay and go. I want to give the one who was hired last the same as I gave you. Don't I have the right to do what I want with my own money? Or are you envious because I am generous?' So the last will be first, and the first will be last." (Matthew 20:1–16)

When I visited my ailing father in Coptic Hospital, Nairobi, he always displayed the image of a jovial man, despite his sickness, and he would ask me to sing with him. He knew very many Christian songs. This helped me not to pity him as he approached his final days but rather to be content that he was going to live eternally with Christ after life on earth.

One day we visited him with my mum, Rhoda. She seemed to pity him. She also looked visibly scared. But Mzee opened his eyes and encouraged her to remain strong. "Do not fear anything about me. Whatever will happen is the will of God, and I'm prepared for it," he said from his bed.

Mzee Daudi was born in 1924 in Muumandu village, Machakos. He went to Tala Salvation school in 1931 and completed the common entrance level exam. He worked as a carpenter specializing in fitting cushions on chairs. Later on, he trained as a painter and worked for many years in numerous companies in Nairobi, Molo and even Central Kenya. He was blessed with 10 children: Charles Mulli, Harrison Musyoka, Stephen Dickson, Zacharia Mulwa, Job Kaleli, Samson Lila, Joshua Nzuki, Joel Ndambuki, Miriam Muthikwa and Peter Muithi. He was buried in Ngei village, Ndalani, on March 12, 2015. We thanked God for the many years that He had enabled us to live with our father.

As I reflect on my own role as a father I see there is something very unique in being the mentor of so many children. I carry so much on my shoulders. I work tirelessly. And I serve ceaselessly. If I were to fail to stand as a father, I am sure I would feel awful. I need to meet the many obligations I have in being a father. Even though a father is honoured by the way he treats his children and provides for them, it is still a big challenge to meet this standard.

As a father I take responsibility for the whole organization. Being a father means commitment. It is real commitment with love. There is no giving up. There is no running away. It is a marathon. You keep going. You stand strong in the Lord and trust in Him. God honours this commitment, and He works to restore hope in the family.

My life has never been easy in any way. I did not have the advantage of building off of a good father. I learned nothing from my father. He was really cruel. So how could I bring up my family in a Christian way of life? I had to learn the hard way. I learned good Christian values in my life, and I trusted God to teach me to be a good father to what some call the biggest family in the world.

Being a father is no easy task. Sometimes as parents we face the difficult challenges of wayward children. It can be a difficult and trying experience. Children have run away from MCF, and I have taken the time to go back and look for them and bring them back. Change does not always happen as fast as we want. The key with wayward children is to be patient. This is important in the role of a parent. In the dilemma of difficult children, patience pays a great return. Persevering in prayer, being ready to forgive and always staying in love brings honour to God. In this way, the father plays the role helping to transform the child.

And above all, pray together with children with the assurance that God hears us when we call on Him and acts to bring restoration.

Chapter Thirteen
THE ART OF PHILANTHROPY

Philanthropy is about giving. We tend to think of it as the art of serving the less fortunate in society by providing education, shelter, food, water and medical care. And all of this is good. Yet the deeper aspect of philanthropy, the aspect by which philanthropy can truly be characterized, is not so much *what* is done but *why* it is done.

The Collins English Dictionary defines philanthropy as "love of mankind" and "the practice of performing charitable or benevolent actions." It is this love for mankind that enables people to give to charity. This love compels people to be their brothers' keeper.

The motivation for philanthropy is that it comes from a willing giver. Not under compulsion. It should extend from someone whose heart wants to provide. From someone who wants to give without expecting anything in return.

In business you build so that you can gain. But in philanthropy you build in order for someone else to gain. Instead of constructing on behalf of yourself, you construct on behalf of the community.

A true philanthropist is free from wanting anything in return. No fame. No recognition. In fact, you give and sometimes people don't even know that you did anything. Jesus says, "But when you give to the needy, do not let your left hand know what your right hand is doing, so that your giving may be in secret. Then your Father, who sees what is done in secret, will reward you" (Matthew 6:3–4).

My philanthropic work started when I became drawn in by the needs of the people. I saw the need, and I responded. I helped those who were in a desperate situation, a collapsed economy and a dying community. They needed help, and by the grace of God I helped. It is not much more complicated than that.

Philanthropic work involves assessing the situation of a given people and becoming convinced that they need help. Your heart is moved. You are not able to ignore those who have impacted you. And you become consumed with a desire to lift them higher. To get them out of the pit they are in.

People should give because their hearts are generous. Their hearts get motivated to give by the need they see. And when you see a need, when your heart loves the person in trouble, and when you selflessly take action to help that person, then you are philanthropic.

And this love is your inspiration. You never get tired, because you start with your heart. You give even when you don't have enough. You start giving with your heart, and then it flows to material giving. Giving is not about your material possessions. It is the ability to take initiative and to go forth and act.

Yet not everyone sees it this way.

One of the challenges in Africa is that people want to help their own families and not others. There is a persistent problem with egotism and self-ishness. People want their own tribe and their own families to succeed. It's so hard for them to give to anyone else. This attitude is a disease. It's an African disease. People grab things for themselves. They take more and more and never get satisfied. If things were different, if people desired to help others instead of themselves, Africa would be very far by now.

So why do people keep money for themselves? I ask myself, *What will they do with all of it?* A strange cycle develops where people amass more and more wealth and never ask themselves why they are doing it.

Africans will invest their money in the West, but how hard it is for them to invest in their fellow Africans. The Bible says to love your neighbour. But when people rise up, they don't want to part with their riches. The money clouds their vision, blinds them. They become consumed with their desire for money. They want power and wealth to be able to dominate. This drives them crazy. They want so much, so they oppress others and put them down.

In Kenya and even across the world, we have many once-upon-a-time poor boys and girls who are now millionaires and even billionaires. But because they do not have a giving heart and the love for humankind, as commanded by God, they do not give anything back to society. Instead, they seek to acquire more and more. It becomes their only goal in life.

This is why many people in Kenya think of me as a stupid person. They think I am a fool. I am bringing tribes together. But in the African mindset, I am *supposed* to concentrate on my own tribe and build up only them. What I do is contrary to what other people think I should do.

When I started MCF and helped many street children and other needy groups, I could see that many people link these acts of kindness with my childhood. Those who had heard my life history concluded that I was giving to the poor because I was also born poor. They believed that I chose to focus on street children because I was just like them during my childhood.

I have compassion for the poor because I understand what they are going through. But not all who grow up poor and later become rich are able to look back and help the needy. Loving others is a question of the condition of your heart, not of your wallet. Some people believe that you must be extremely rich in order to give, but I disagree. Giving is all about your heart. You do not need to be a millionaire to love humankind. You do not need millions of dollars to practice benevolence. We have so many rich people who give little to society, and we have so many ordinary people who give a lot to society. People do not give because they have much; they give because they have a big heart.

Real philanthropy is when we are touched by the disadvantaged situations others are in, when we are willing to act out of love to do whatever is needed. It just takes an ordinary person to make a difference in the life of another ordinary person. As co-workers of Christ, our work is to shoulder each other's burden. As we look to the cross, Christ will change our hearts. Even our Lord was not a rich person. Yet He gave more than anyone else. And it is His life, His generosity, His wisdom and His passion that enables us to love people with a fervent love.

In my opinion, every person should be involved in philanthropy. Each of us should lift up the poor. Why? Because the things we have are not ours. We are custodians of God's wealth. Why would we think that what we have belongs to us? The Bible says, "What do you have that you did not receive? And if you did receive it, why do you boast as though you did not?" (1 Corinthians 4:7). We came into this world with nothing, and one day we will leave with nothing. I witnessed this with my brother's death. I looked into the coffin, and there was only a body, a suit, a tie and shoes. There was no money. This is the case for everyone. You come with nothing, and you leave with nothing. What matters is what you give during your time on earth.

The Bible says, "Where your treasure is, there your heart will be also" (Matthew 6:21). Our bank account is a big issue. Do we trust God there? Or do we secretly keep that away from God? Is our bank account our source of security? Are we afraid that we will be left abandoned by God, so we stockpile as much as we can so that we can feel the false sense of security that money brings?

The heart of giving is very special. You really can give without measure. The Provider knows that as you give, He will provide you with more to give. When I give to others, I give everything. There are many needs. There are so many children. But nothing will stop me from giving what is within my reach to give. God will give, provided you have no interest in something for yourself. He will give if you want something for someone else. It's not about us. God gives so that you can give to others. Then God opens His hands in a more dynamic way to bless the effort you have made.

After God blessed me with a job and later as my numerous businesses grew tremendously, I always felt that I owed Him everything that I possessed. I had risen from the life of a pauper to become a millionaire, and I knew that it was only through God's mercy that I had come thus far. All I had was His.

With the spirit of saying thank you to the Lord, I decided to start giving back to society as a way of appreciating God. These are some of the principles and convictions that led me into philanthropy and to eventually start MCF in Eldoret, which would later grow into big centres in Yatta and Ndalani. I knew that God gives, and He uses those whom He has blessed with wealth to reach out to others.

❀ ❀ ❀

Curiously, philanthropy is as beneficial to the donor as to the recipient. However little you give, as long as it is from deep down in your heart and given with love you will get a strong feeling of contentment. Personally, I have experienced this when I discover that the small assistance I extended to the needy somewhere has been able to make a huge difference in their lives. It makes me happy.

The driving force behind my commitment to philanthropic work is out of a divine conviction to reach out to the underprivileged by giving back to society.

In 2012, I was greatly impressed by an annual theme at the Christ Is the Answer Ministries in Kenya, which said, "Reach each one." This was a simple but very effective statement about reaching many people so that each one of them can embrace salvation. For instance, if a congregation has 1,000 people and each person reaches out to one other person, the number of saved people will increase by 1,000. The same applies to philanthropy. If each one of us can reach one other person with the little that we have, then a lot of resources will be given out and we will not have poor and destitute children in this country. We shall have more to share and will even have a surplus. For instance, if one million Kenyans purpose to save one street child each, then the street children problem can be eradicated in Kenya in a day! It is as simple as it sounds.

I engage in philanthropy because I believe in the hidden potential of the vulnerable children and groups. I believe that the underprivileged can move from nothing to something if empowered through best practices. Much of philanthropic work depends not only on what you see but on what you think is possible. That child wearing smelly clothes and eating from a garbage bin can become a medical doctor. Does that sound impossible? That girl standing on a street corner late at night, forced to be there by her parents, can become a social worker who loves and reforms many young girls. Does that sound impossible? Nothing is impossible to those who believe. The greatest blessing any of us can have is faith in God. And God enables us to see. He enables us to see not simply what is but what can be.

People saw Peter as a simple fisherman. Jesus saw a future apostle who would be mighty in His kingdom. People saw Saul as a murderous tyrant. Jesus saw a faithful follower who would write much of the New Testament. What do you see? Our God will give us eyes to see.

As philanthropists, we invest in people. We are the people who can make a positive difference, the people who can make a positive change, the people who can make the world a better place. The more you help people to better their lives, the more you advance God's plans for humankind.

Furthermore, my philanthropic work is aimed at creating opportunities for the less privileged in society so as to avoid seeing them degenerate into crime and other social ills. In many cases, when a section of society feels neglected, it resorts to committing crimes against the rich in the society. When we support the cause to reach out to the less fortunate, we participate in turning away anger, hatred and criminal tendencies from our society and moulding the people into loving, humane and responsible members of society. Any amount of resources and any form of giving that facilitates the touching of lives eventually help society in fighting crime, ignorance and poverty.

However, before engaging in philanthropy, you should examine your motives for venturing into philanthropic service. The goal of philanthropy should not be personal gain but should be that of helping to create a difference in the lives of others, especially the less fortunate in society. And while giving, you should always remain consistent, dedicated and true to the cause, even when faced with challenges. You may not feel appreciated by the recipients, but this should not discourage you from giving.

In 2012, I was recognized by a philanthropy awards body known as the East Africa Association of Grantmakers (EAAG) in a ceremony held in Entebbe, Uganda. I was honoured for initiating and setting up a family foundation that has demonstrated an outstanding commitment to philanthropy through direct financial support and that has encouraged others to take philanthropic leadership roles in communities. In recognition of MCF's outstanding contribution to strategic social development and the growth of philanthropy in East Africa, I received the Family Philanthropy Award. The CEO of EAAG, Mr. Nicanor Sabula, said that the organization being given the award represents the best example of organized giving with a focus on sustainability for holistic transformation. He reiterated that philanthropy is not about good intentions only but about the impact arising from the vision and mission.

The key principle that has guided our work for the last 25 years is nondiscrimination in our programs. We ensure that we are not guided by religious or tribal viewpoints but rather that every child should have the rights he or she deserves, regardless of skin colour, tribe or religion. We show pure, unconditional Christian love to all children, while at the same time exhibiting a high sense of integrity, honesty, accountability and transparency. Anyone wishing to focus on the rescue and rehabilitation of vulnerable children must be ready to provide unconditional love and undivided attention to all children, irrespective of their behaviour and attitudes or even their family status. MCF has been able to touch many children without discrimination.

At the end of the day my satisfaction comes from seeing the extreme transformation in the lives of children and vulnerable adults. As they eventually reintegrate into society, they transition from a life of lack, want, suffering and hopelessness to a state of independence and confidence, leading a dignified life. Every time I walk around the MCF homes, especially in Yatta and Ndalani, I feel so happy to see the lives of young child mothers from different backgrounds who were forced into motherhood become defined by hope, determination, self-worth and love as they raise the very children who marked their misery and neglect.

The transformed lives enable people to see MCF as a trusted steward for empowering the poor, restoring hope, nurturing dreams and creating a peaceful and responsible world citizenry.

However, in the last 25 years of working directly with needy people and communities, I have come to believe that the biggest transformation needed in our societies is the transformation of a person's mind. If we get rid of negative mindsets and attitudes from other people, all the rest will be possible to achieve in life. The biggest engine that propels humanity is the mind. In most cases, our people in Africa have wrong mindsets. They believe that most things around them are impossible. They get defeated and give up prematurely, even before attempting something. Others do not believe in themselves. They presume that it takes someone else to do something better and do not believe they can do it themselves.

Furthermore, due to poor leadership, the people have been encouraged to wait for handouts from politicians. This has created a culture of dependence. As a result, we have slept on our potential and embraced this wrong culture of leadership. At MCF, I hold regular meetings with children and encourage them to be independent in their pursuit for greatness. I tell them not to fear to try something. I encourage them to do anything, however small, so that they make their own money and stop waiting to be helped. We empower and transform their minds through participatory education that nurtures a positive attitude. We tell them to avoid prejudices and premature conclusions and to take things the way they come. We further advise them to learn from the best, be optimistic and shun pessimistic thoughts.

When children have a positive change in their attitude and experience the strengthening of their self-esteem, their confidence in their abilities is enhanced. This enables them to take ownership of the long-term positive change in their lives and society. For instance, microenterprise training, Christian values, volunteer service and social ethics are common courses in all MCF rehabilitation and training programs for children, which prepare them for the accountable use of resources when they exit from institutional care.

Holistic transformation through parental care, psychosocial support, proper nutrition, spiritual nourishment, education, vocational training, developing of talent through sports, mentoring, empowerment and participation in community work has been key in the exposure and overall transformation of the lives in the communities. We encourage the creation of employment and opportunities that empower communities to take charge of their lives, resulting in social change.

I am glad that children who went through MCF have gone out there and made a huge difference in their own lives and the lives of others. They have created opportunities for themselves and even others.

In the spirit of giving, the Almighty God sent His only begotten Son that whoever believes in Him should not perish but have eternal life. The act of giving started when God saw the need. He is the greatest philanthropist. He gave to us His great love. We follow the footsteps of the Lord Jesus Christ. We can do the same to love others, and in so doing we love God.

In all of this, God never demanded that we pay Him back. Indeed, we could not pay Him back. Thankfully, the debt was paid by Jesus.

This incredible love of God frees us from the need to promote ourselves. We become thrilled that we know Jesus. And this opens our hearts and our eyes to see and work towards a bright future for the benefit of others.

I believe that many of us have the capacity to support others, but we are often afraid of getting involved. We rate our capacity as being too inconsequential to make a difference in the lives of others. We have bought into the notion that our small efforts are not useful and that someone else could do it so much better than us, so why bother? But the little boy with the five loaves and two fish did not see it that way. It is not about what you have but what you give. That little boy gave everything he had to Jesus. And Jesus used what was in His hands.

Chapter Fourteen
OUR DIVINE CALLING EXPANDS
Mully University

God has accomplished much through the ministry of MCF, and I always think about how our expanding ministry at MCF can be sustained. I ask God where He wants us to go in the future and what needs we should respond to as we move forward. And fulfilling the vision requires a sustainability plan that includes financial resources as well as capable people to serve in many areas.

Sustainability is important to MCF because it enables us to do everything we can to feed and educate the children and meet other needs so that we do not live in a hopeless situation. One way we are continually blessed is that many of the children who finish the program at MCF choose to stay and help the next generation of rescued children. This helps sustain the personnel needed in the organization.

One example of the human sustainability at MCF is the story of Muthoni. I met Muthoni while helping her and her siblings at the displaced persons camp in Eldoret. She had no father, and her mother was not well. When the time came for us to leave the displaced persons camp, she and her siblings had nowhere to go. But the government insisted that they leave.

I began recruiting over 400 boys and girls who had completed their grade 8 level and had qualified to go to high school. Muthoni told me that she did not want to be left in Eldoret. Like so many girls, she was scared about what might happen to her if she had to go to the streets, so I arranged to rescue her and her siblings. Muthoni had become pregnant as a result of rape during the war and gave birth at the displaced persons camp. Her situation was desperate.

I brought Muthoni and her child to MCF. She had a desire to help the little children at MCF by washing clothes. She worked with us for eight years and later met a man and brought him to MCF. They became engaged, and he began working in the building and construction department. Both of them want to continue at MCF.

There are so many children who decide to stay with us at MCF when they finish, while others move on to study at university or carry on with careers. Either way, it gives me such joy to see my children serving others with all their heart. They are not making their way in the world to benefit themselves. They are seeking to love and serve their fellow man. Those who choose to stay at MCF are called to help the next generation of children. There are so many who have been rescued, and now they are rescuing others. Freely, freely you have received. Freely, freely give. There is no fame or fortune for them at MCF. They, like the others who have gone on to other careers, have discovered what I discovered.

We are here for such a short season. And if we keep eternity in mind, if we see with our spiritual eyes, we will see the joy of letting everything go and simply surrendering all to God for Him to work in us and through us. What does it profit a man if he gains the whole world yet forfeits his soul? It profits him nothing, because he was blinded by the futile and temporal gains of this world. I was taught how to see. And I seek to teach my children how to see.

When they leave MCF, they leave with varying skills and abilities. Yet they have in common the ability to see past earthly gains. They see that whatever gifts they have been given are for the common good. I had to see that my gifts were not meant for me. They were meant to be shared. And as I look at all the good that has happened, I see how this is spreading and multiplying.

When I see rescued children staying, I know this means that our ministry will not only exist for a particular period of time but will continue to serve many needy people for generations to come. MCF remains committed to improving the quality of care services. Our ongoing desire is to facilitate the full transformation of rescued children by supporting them through the years until they acquire the highest level of education and training based on their ability.

Another aspect of sustainability is to always have a vision for the future. Our expansion to other counties in Kenya and to the people of

Tanzania is a reflection of God's call for us to touch as many lives as possible. I believe that MCF will, with time, expand to all African countries and the entire world. We believe that with God everything is possible.

At MCF, we keep praying for God to enable us to continue serving His people for many years and generations to come. We want to touch as many hearts as possible and make a positive difference in their lives. While our focus has been on rehabilitation, primary and secondary education and vocational training, we intend to grow and diversify our activities by also engaging in the provision of university education.

I consider higher education a key component in improving one's life. Education has stood out as the greatest pillar of socioeconomic development in the world. Countries that have invested heavily in education have managed to cross the poverty barrier from being a so-called underdeveloped nation to a developed nation.

With education being one of the fundamental factors of development, no society can achieve sustainable economic development without substantial investment in well-trained human capital. The degree of literacy in a country determines its level of economic growth. Education sharpens people's understanding of themselves and the world; it gives them the ability to innovate and to understand the existing systems of production; it improves their thinking capacity; and generally education improves the quality of lives.

MCF therefore seeks to scale up its efforts to increase opportunities for needy students to access college and university education by establishing Mully University. This institution will target youths in Kenya, especially those from vulnerable backgrounds, for quality professional and entrepreneurial skills training that will enhance their ability to access gainful employment. This Christian university, which will be located in MCF Yatta, will develop, empower and nurture youth and other learners in various professional fields to become servant leaders and persons of integrity in the world.

As we laid down plans to start this unique university in Yatta, I consulted widely with people in the education sector to learn more about establishing and running an institution of higher learning. I also sought advice from my friends in other parts of the world.

I talked to Professor Peter Kibas, a close friend of mine who was serving as vice-chancellor in one of the universities in Nairobi, and sought technical input on how to establish and run a private university. He talked to me at length about the importance of venturing into higher education because at MCF we believed in education as the best mode of rehabilitation. He told me that the demand for higher education in Kenya had grown and continues to grow over the years.

He gave me a long history of the development of higher education in Kenya. His main focus was a university that offers quality education. He said,

> "As we speak now, Kenya has over 60 universities; 22 public universities, 9 public constituent colleges and 30 private universities as of 2015. This number is expected to increase due to a number of institutions having already submitted various applications for charters, elevation to university colleges and acquisition of interim letters of authority. However, as you think of starting a university, your focus should be the quality of education and not the number of students. The quality of graduates you produce is what defines you."

Professor Kibas went on to describe how a university as an institution is expected to take the lead in the development process of a given nation. This would require relating training to the needs of the nation and focusing research on problems related to the reality of the country, its people and its needs.

Even though the number of Kenyan institutions of higher learning today may seem high compared to the initial seven public universities that existed in 2002, the level of students' admission is still low when compared to the high number of candidates who finish secondary school with good grades. Many students cannot access higher education due to lack of resources. And that was one of the issues driving me to make a difference. By seeking to establish a university, I was also looking for an avenue of providing an opportunity for the less fortunate to access education and training at minimal cost.

While chiefly concerned with students' intellectual development, the MCF University will support their moral and spiritual growth and enhance the learners' capacity for leadership through extracurricular programs like sports, singing, dancing and drama. This ensures that our graduates meet the spiritual needs of their clients wherever they go to serve, as teachers, lawyers, community development officers, doctors, nurses or whatever other roles they have in society. Thus my plan is to set up an institution that will develop not only the minds of the learners but also their hearts. I am looking at a highly practical Christian university.

On Sunday, March 15, 2015, the MCF fraternity held prayers and commissioned members of a task force that is mandated to put in place the relevant structures, curriculum and policies that will ensure the university's smooth launch. The prayers were conducted by Bishop Mulandi, Rev. Dr. Titus Kivunzi and myself. During the event, I expressed optimism that everything is possible with God. I told the gathering that MCF had embarked on an ambitious project of establishing a Christian university, and I believe that we will succeed because God is on our side. I called on well-wishers to pray for this noble course.

We ask God to lead the way as we embark on establishing an institution that will help shape minds and impart youth with the right knowledge that will enable them to serve God effectively as intellectuals. This institution is aimed at increasing higher learning opportunities for MCF beneficiaries as well as other deserving students. In this regard, MCF is making great strides in terms of championing the academic development of its beneficiaries, who were once hopeless.

We will be a leader in child and community development. The university will also seek to revolutionize research and technology transfer in climate change mitigation and adaptation, social entrepreneurship, modern agriculture, and social science. As a centre of knowledge that will continue to expand its area of studies, our university is expected to provide informed advice on various matters regarding the development of the nation, including science and technology and social, economic, political and other issues.

Many universities are being opened across the country, both private and public, but a lot of strategic planning needs to be put in place to ensure that these learning institutions are able to offer the best to the students and the country. By 2015, there were over 60 universities operating in Kenya. However, the MCF University seeks to be unique by embracing the principles of "I see. I learn. I practice. I disseminate." God, in His power, will make this dream a reality.

Chapter Fifteen

YOUR JOURNEY OF FAITH

Each of us wants our life to count. Each of us wants to know that our time here has mattered. Deep down inside we want the assurance that we have fulfilled our purpose. No one wants to walk through life aimlessly. So how can we have this assurance?

The ruler Nicodemus came to Jesus at night. He wanted to talk with Him. Jesus gave him these famous words: "For God so loved the world that he gave his one and only Son, that whoever believes in him shall not perish but have eternal life" (John 3:16).

To believe in Jesus gives complete hope. And yet sometimes we can misunderstand these words to think that they only mean we get to go to heaven after we die.

Jesus also said, "I have come that they may have life, and have it to the full" (John 10:10). If we believe in Jesus, we will want to surrender our lives here on earth to Him. We will want to walk with Him while we are here. We will want to live with His purpose.

I believe in Jesus. I have turned my life over to Him. Knowing that I am walking right down the centre of the path with my Lord and Saviour gives me the greatest sense of purpose.

We are all called to live by His power day by day and moment by moment. And the way in which God will work through us is different for each person. I have my calling. And so do you.

Ephesians 2:10 says, "For we are God's handiwork, created in Christ Jesus to do good works, which God prepared in advance for us to do."

God prepared works for you and I to do well before we were born. We are not saved by the works we do. Not me. Not anyone. I am not saved by the work I do in rescuing children. I am saved only by the precious blood of Jesus Christ. That is why now I can be used by God to carry out His works that He has planned for me to do.

And the works that I do—all of them—are His doing.

As I look back on my life, my opinion is that no one thinks of me as a businessman anymore. There is nothing wrong with business. I enjoyed being in business. I only say that when people hear the name Charles Mulli their thought is that this is the man who follows Jesus and helps all those African children.

The reason I mention this is because we may think we know where we are going in life. I thought I did. I thought business was it, even though in my heart I knew something was not right. Proverbs says, "There is a way that appears to be right, but in the end it leads to death" (Proverbs 14:12). Only God knows the right path for us. And this does not come by trying to force God to do things our way. It comes by surrendering and listening to God's call.

Bring them all back to Me.

Yet when we hear God's call, we can become concerned and worried about what might happen to our lives. We can become fearful at the thought of having to give up control. This is why it is important to understand that control is an illusion. And it is in surrendering to Jesus that we actually discover life in Him. Jesus says, "Whoever finds their life will lose it, and whoever loses their life for my sake and the gospel will find it" (Matthew 10:39).

There were many people who wanted to join Jesus on a journey of faith. But they were afraid of what would happen to them. Fear kept them from trusting Him. The rich young ruler wanted to follow Jesus, but he could not imagine his life without his possessions. And so he turned back. He hung on to that which he would not be able to keep in eternity anyway.

When I gave up all my wealth and all my businesses, there were many who thought I was truly crazy. But now, people have been able to see that I am walking with God. I was not only willing to believe in Jesus for eternal life, but I also accepted His call to live how He wants me to live during my time here on earth.

Acts 20:24 says, "However, I consider my life worth nothing to me; my only aim is to finish the race and complete the task the Lord Jesus has given me—the task of testifying to the good news of God's grace."

I was willing by the grace of God to follow the course He set before me. I was willing, over time, to completely surrender and say, "Here I am, Lord; send me."

And my question to you is, are you willing to be used by God for His purposes?

Are you willing to allow Jesus to lead you on your journey of faith with Him?

I have heard people say that they could never do what I am doing. I can tell you that not even I think I can do what I am doing. Really, when I look at everything around me, it is like a dream world. To have the privilege of helping children every day and seeing their lives transformed, to see the MCF locations with their many buildings and farms—it is nothing short of a miracle.

But the results are from God's hands. Not mine. This was the work I was given to do. It is far too impossible for any one person to do. For me, I see it as obvious that it is only by Almighty God that this work is possible. How could one man do this? Totally impossible for man. But what is impossible with man is possible with God. I did not choose to do this work. I did not sit down one day and make God a proposal. He said this was His will for me.

And I said yes.

You have your calling as well. God wants to work through you to complete the works He called you to walk in. You have your work to do. And there are no bigger or smaller callings in God's kingdom. Because we live on this earth we sometimes think in terms of different kinds of work being more important and less important. This thinking is not correct.

There are no greater or lesser callings with God. There is only faithful and unfaithful. The apostle Paul had his ministry, and the shepherds who came to visit Jesus at His birth had their ministry. Both were faithful to what God called them to do. And it is God who makes everything work together for good for His glory. My prayer for you is that you, too, would be willing to say, "Yes, God, here I am. Send me," in whatever His plans are for you.

My journey of faith with Jesus is the most amazing, most thrilling adventure I could ever know. He is a faithful God. His promises are yes and amen. When things in my life looked their darkest, when I really looked around and could not see any solution, He was there to continue His work in me. Wherever you cannot see, that's where God is.

There are times in life when we cannot see the answer. We may think, *Where is God? Where has He gone?* He is right there. In that place where you think it is all lost, He is there. When you feel like you have no hope, that is where God comes in. You see God after you have hit the wall. You are completely exhausted. You cannot depend on yourself. God takes us to these places so that we come to the end of ourselves. God will bring us to that place so that we can see that we are not clever. Someone may be depending on themselves, their skills, or even their addictions. They think, *Nothing can harm me.* But when we really need help, then God is there.

He will be faithful to you as you carry out His calling. He loves you. He cares for you. He is thrilled with you. The God of all heaven has total joy in you.

When I go to the streets, the children need to be convinced that I love them. They come from such difficult backgrounds. They have tried to find relief from their problems in many difficult ways. It takes time for them to see the love God has for them. And when the children let go of their fears and accept the love of Christ, they too begin their journey of faith.

I could have stayed in business. There is not one person who would have faulted me for staying in business. But as I look at all the children who have been rescued, I would not trade any amount of money or fame for them. I do not regret walking with Jesus. Not even one minute.

It is true that a journey of faith has challenges. There are those who hope that Jesus will give them an easy life. A life without difficulties. A life without problems. But this is not a reasonable way to approach a life of faith. The disciples did not have it easy. Even our Lord did not have it easy. When situations become difficult, we might want to walk away from the battle because we fear defeat. The Israelites were afraid of Goliath until David came and routed the enemy. And Jesus says, "In the world you will have trouble. But take heart! I have overcome the world" (John 16:33). So we need to recognize that difficulties will come. But God is greater than our difficulties.

Let each of us be encouraged that with Jesus we are always victorious. His banner over us is love. He will enable us to love our enemies. He will enable us to love those who cannot return the favour. He will enable us to see the need He has called us to fill and to risk everything to respond to that need. He will enable us to believe every word He has spoken. He will open our eyes to see as He sees.

He will enable us to live our journey of faith.

FATHER TO THE
FATHERLESS

The Charles Mulli Story

PAUL H. BOGE
Foreword by Bruce Wilkinson, *Dream for Africa*

The Children. The Calling. The Compassion.

HOPE FOR THE
HOPELESS
The Charles Mulli Mission

PAUL H. BOGE

Foreword by David Rowlands

Introduction by H.E. Hon. Daniel Arap Moi, Second President of the Republic of Kenya